James River Guide

Insiders' Paddling and Fishing Trips from Headwaters Down to Richmond

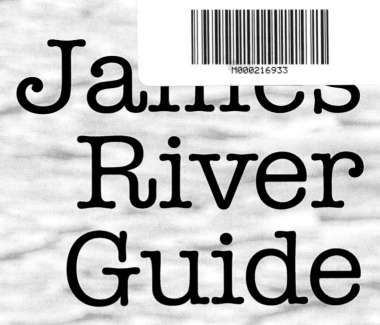

Bruce Ingram

Includes Coverage of the Maury, Seven New Trips, and Updated How-To and River Access Info

The author gratefully acknowledges permission
from the Virginia Canals & Navigations Society (VaCanals.org)
to adapt four maps for the third edition of this book.

Secant Publishing, LLC
615 N. Pinehurst Ave.
Salisbury, MD 21801
SecantPublishing.com

Previous edition published by Ecopress, 2007

The chapter entitled "Classic Fishing Lures that Have Stood the Test of Time,"
which is new to the Third Edition of this book, is reprinted with permission from *Outdoor America,*
the official publication of the Izaak Walton League of America, where it first appeared.

ISBN: 978-0-9904608-5-5
ISBN (mobi) 978-0-9907833-2-9
ISBN (epub) 978-0-9907833-1-2

Photography by Bruce Ingram
Cover and interior by Rebecca Finkel, F + P Graphic Design

Printed in the United States of America
1   2   3   4   5   6   7   8   9   10

Dear Thomas,

The James is my favorite river. I hope my book helps you explore the waterway

Best,

Bruce Ingram

August 26, 2017

James River Overview

Headwaters

Trip Start	Trip Complete	Miles	Class Rapids	Map
1 Iron Gate	Gala	9	3	48
2 Gala	Eagle Rock	4	0	58
3 Eagle Rock	Narrow Passage	13	2	62
4 Narrow Passage	Springwood	3	1	70
5 Springwood	Buchanan	4	0	76
6 Buchanan	Arcadia	6	2	76
7 Arcadia	Alpine	4.5	1	84
8 Alpine	Glasgow	10.5	3	90
9 Glasgow	Snowden	5.5	Balcony Falls III+	90

The James Between the Dams

Trip Start	Trip Complete	Miles	Class Rapids	Map
10 Bedford Dam	Bedford Dam	1.5	0	98
11 Bedford Dam	Hunting Creek	3	Braidel Channel	102
12 Reed Creek	Big Island Dam	0.75	0	102

Upper James

Trip Start	Trip Complete	Miles	Class Rapids	Map
13 Scotts Mill Dam	Six Mile Bridge	6	0	110
14 Six Mile Bridge	Joshua Falls	4	0	110
15 Joshua Falls	Riverville	16	1+	118
16 Riverville	Bent Creek	2.5	0	126
17 Bent Creek	Wingina	12.5	0	130
18 Wingina	James R.W.M.A.	2.5	0	134
19 James R.W.M.A.	Howardsville	10	2	134
20 Howardsville	Scottsville	11	1+	142

Middle James

Trip Start	Trip Complete	Miles	Class Rapids	Map
21 Scottsville	Hardware River	6	0	148
22 Hardware River	Bremo Bluff	7	2+	154
23 Bremo Bluff	Columbia	11	0	158
24 Columbia	Cartersville	9.5	0	164
25 Cartersville	West View	5	0	164
26 West View	Maidens	11.5	0	170
27 Maidens	Watkins Landing	13	0	174
28 Watkins Landing	Huguenot Flatwater	10	0	178
29 Huguenot Flatwater	Ancarrow's Landing	9	multiple Class II+ rapids	180

Contents

Introduction vii

Section One: Recreation Opportunities 1

Fishing the James 3

Let Ledges Give You the Edge 7

Going Soft for Smallmouths 12

Falling For Autumn River Bass 17

How To Hook Panfish, Catfish, and Muskies 20

Floating the James 24

Why Conservation Easements Make Sense 28

Classic Fishing Lures that Have Stood the Test of Time . . 35

The Marvelous Maury River:
    The Upper James River's Main Tributary 42

Section Two: The Headwaters 47

1 Iron Gate to Gala 48

2 Gala to Eagle Rock 57

3 Eagle Rock to Narrow Passage 62

4 Narrow Passage to Springwood 70

5 Springwood to Buchanan 75

6 Buchanan to Arcadia 80

7 Arcadia to Alpine 84

8 Alpine to Glasgow 89

9 Glasgow to Snowden 94

Section Three: The James Between the Dams 97

10 Bedford Dam to Bedford Dam 98

11 Bedford Dam to Hunting Creek 102

12 Reed Creek to Big Island Dam and Back 106

Section Four: Upper James 109

  13 Scotts Mill Dam to Six-Mile Bridge 110

  14 Six-Mile Bridge (Lynchburg) to Joshua Falls 114

  15 Joshua Falls to Riverville 117

  16 Riverville to Bent Creek 125

  17 Bent Creek to Wingina 129

  18 Wingina to James River WMA 134

  19 James River WMA to Howardsville 138

  20 Howardsville to Scottsville 142

Section Five: Middle James 147

  21 Scottsville to Hardware River WMA 148

  22 Hardware River WMA to Bremo Bluff 153

  23 Bremo Bluff to Columbia 158

  24 Columbia to Cartersville 163

  25 Cartersville to West View 167

  26 West View to Maidens 170

  27 Maidens to Watkins Landing 174

  28 Watkins Landing to Huguenot Flatwater 177

  29 Huguenot Flatwater to Ancarrow's Landing 180

Appendix A: Trip Planner 184

Index 187

Introduction

As a lifelong resident of southwest Virginia, I have an enduring fascination with the James River. But the river is not just for those who reside in one section of the Old Dominion. Over ninety percent of the state's population lives less than a three-hour drive from the James, and it is no wonder that this waterway often dominates the state fishing and canoeing scenes.

The James has long been one of the most popular waterways in the Mid-Atlantic, and communities are beginning to take notice. The Botetourt County Office of Tourism (the river begins in this county) along with local businesses and citizens helped design The Upper James River Water Trail as a way of promoting the river and its charms.

John Mays, co-owner of Twin River Outfitters in Buchanan, describes the special nature of this section.

"The Upper James River and its tributaries offer paddlers over a hundred river miles of great trip options to suit every skill level and interest," he said. "There are trips for fishermen, white water adventure seekers, overnight canoe campers, lazy river paddlers, and those just looking to enjoy the great wilderness views. The Upper James River features great mountain scenery, some exciting rapids, lots of wildlife viewing opportunities all in the rural setting of the Blue Ridge Mountains of Virginia.

"With a few exceptions, the majority of the Upper James features easy class I and II rapids making it ideal for paddling recreational kayaks or canoes. With the Upper James River Water Trail & Alleghany High-lands Blueway initiatives, lots of new river access points have been added, with even more planned, making accessing the river easier than ever."

For ease of reference, I have divided the area of the James this book covers into three sections: the James' Headwaters (Iron Gate to Snowden) the James between the Dams; the Upper James (Scotts Mill Dam to Scottsville); and the Middle James (Scottsville to Anacarrow's Landing). Seven dams interrupt the river from Snowden to Lynchburg and I cover only the float trips possible on the upper reaches. I wish that people could canoe the entire upper river, but sadly they cannot because of a lack of accessibility. I resume my coverage at Scotts Mill Dam in Lynchburg and continue until the James turns tidal at Ancarrow's Landing in the Richmond area.

Fishing is a major aspect of this work, and the book particularly covers how and where to angle for smallmouth bass. Although people journey to the upper river to seek out various species of gamefish, the smallmouth is by far the most eagerly pursued fish. A look at sporting magazines verifies the hold this black bass has on anglers. I have found the smallmouth bass to be an endlessly interesting creature that frequently eludes me, but that always draws me back to the river.

Finally, readers should realize that the James, like all rivers, is a living entity, constantly subject to change. The information presented is the most up to date at the time of publication, but floods and other weather-related phenomena can increase or decrease the class of a rapid—even eliminating or creating a stretch of white water. Access points are always subject to change over time. Be sure to check with the canoe liveries and information sources listed in the appendix before planning a trip to an unfamiliar section.

I am a fisherman, canoeist, bird watcher, photographer, and conservationist. My happiest times are spent in the outdoors. Although this book is mainly geared toward the angler and paddler I hope that it will appeal to all outdoor lovers, especially those who want to know the James better.

—BRUCE INGRAM

Upper James River Water Trail: UpperJamesRiverWaterTrail.com
Allegheny Highlands Blueway: AlleghanyHighlandBlueway.com

Recreation Opportunities

Fishing the James 3

Let Ledges Give You the Edge 7

Going Soft for Smallmouths 12

Falling For Autumn River Bass 17

How To Hook Panfish, Catfish, and Muskies . . 20

Floating the James 24

Why Conservation Easements Make Sense . . 28

Classic Fishing Lures that Have Stood
the Test of Time 32

The Marvelous Maury River:
The Upper James River's Main Tributary 42

Fishing The James

The upper James River hosts a number of popular gamefish, but by far the most sought after is the smallmouth bass. Bud LaRoche, a retired regional fisheries manager for the Virginia Department of Game and Inland Fisheries (VDGIF), details why this waterway is often considered the best smallmouth stream in the Old Dominion and one of the premier rivers in the United States.

"I would have to say the number one reason the smallmouth fishing is so good is the availability of good habitat," he says. "Rocks, rubble, cobble bars, and boulders all exist; and the river contains a considerable amount of woody cover and debris. The James also has fine spawning habitat; so typically, unless spring floods occur, good spawns will take place. The river does not have an unusual number of minnow species as some streams do, but it does hold good populations of crayfish and insects."

On the James River, any smallmouth over twenty inches should be considered a trophy. A fish this size may weigh four pounds or more, and every year a few six pounders come from the river. My personal best James smallie weighed five pounds, and I carefully released the fish. Catch-and-release is often the norm among anglers today. Fishermen should especially consider releasing larger fish (those weighing two pounds or more), because they provide an important part of the sport fishery. If anglers want to keep bass for the pan, LaRoche says, the smaller fish (that is, those under ten inches) are the ones that should be creeled. Larger fish are the most prolific spawners.

Muskies are another major gamefish, especially on the upper reaches of the river. In fact, the James and the New rivers are often considered Virginia's top muskie locales. Biologist LaRoche says there is a possibility that this member of the pike family spawns in the upper river, but that the fisheries department believes continued stockings are needed to maintain the species' presence. Muskies are not native to the James.

Muskies are not found throughout the James' headwaters. They typically congregate at the mouths of small tributaries. Another likely place to prospect for this member of the pike family is along shorelines that present plenty of downed logs. Muskies often top thirty inches on the river and specimens over ten pounds are present. However, fishing for muskies requires some of the most specialized tackle and techniques of any freshwater gamefish. They are quite difficult to entice with a bait or lure and are hard to land as well. As large as smallmouths and muskies grow, they are not the largest predators in the river. That distinction goes to the flathead catfish.

"In the early to mid-1970s—there are no official records—some game department personnel moved a handful of flathead catfish from Claytor Lake to the upper James," says LaRoche. "At that time, the individual thought he was doing the right thing, but in hindsight, the transfer probably wasn't the best idea. If a large predator is relocated to a place where it doesn't exist, no one knows what the consequences will be. The biological community has since

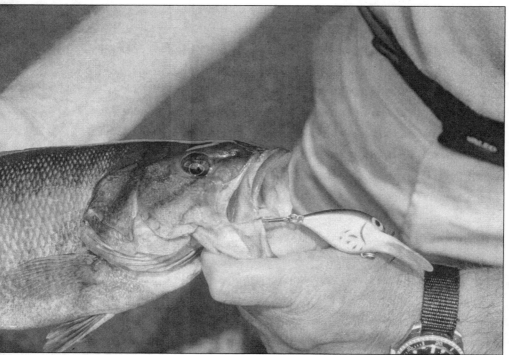

Smallmouth bass are the most sought after species on the James River.

learned that moving non-native predators is not good, but it has been a hard lesson to learn."

The biologist states that "something" has greatly reduced the rock bass and redbreast sunfish populations on the James and, although there are no hard facts to prove blame, flatheads are the prime suspect. LaRoche points out that flatheads prefer sunfish, so circumstantial evidence certainly points in their direction. Channel and bullhead catfish populations are similarly reduced on the James, and flatheads are known to prey on their "cousins" as well.

The flathead can have a negative impact on smallmouth numbers. In decades past, anglers would often report that they caught a hundred bass per day. The plus side to the decrease in bass numbers, though, is that the average size of this species has likely increased over the last 20 years or so. When fewer members of a species inhabit a given stretch of a river, the survivors have access to more food and have higher growth potential. Still, after recovering from the fish kills that afflicted the river in the first decade of the 21th century, the James is as good, if not better, than it ever has been for anglers who like to chase after bigger smallmouths.

Although the introduction of flathead catfish has had some undesirable results, many fishermen have welcomed the arrival of this gamefish. Anglers regularly take flatheads in the twenty-pound range, and thirty pounders appear from time to time. However, relatively few of these huge fish are being weighed in—a situation that LaRoche would like to see change.

"I wish fishermen would keep more of the flatheads they catch," he says. "Of course, there is nothing we can do now to totally remove them from the river, but I wouldn't mind seeing their numbers decrease. In any event, the flathead is a tremendous sport fish. I would like to encourage more people to fish for them."

On the upper river, two hot spots stand out for flatheads. Anglers after this square-tailed catfish generally do not float from point A to B; instead, they employ a motorized johnboat to fish up and down long, deep pools, or they set up camp along a bank that borders these pools. Sandy shorelines are preferred, and campfire rings often dot these banks—a strong clue that good fishing exists.

The focal points for catfish are the Springwood and Buchanan put-ins in Botetourt County. The Springwood access point, located off Route 630 under the Springwood Bridge, features a wide pool on river right, less than a quarter mile below the put-in. This site is favored not only by flathead fanciers, but also by those after muskies and carp. But the Buchanan access point is perhaps most popular with catfish fans. Nearly any summer night, especially on Fridays and Saturdays, anglers line the river-right bank, their rods resting on forked branches lodged in the sand. The more adventurous will motor upstream to the first riffle area—a distance of less than a mile—and then slowly drift downstream. The Buchanan put-in is located in the middle of town, just upstream from the Route 11 Bridge.

Flatheads have been found throughout the freshwater James River from its beginnings in Botetourt County to Richmond. The elongated pools in the area of the James River Wildlife Management Area and between Bent Creek and Wingina are likely places to find this catfish. Still, probably nowhere is the flathead so eagerly sought as at the Buchanan access point.

Carp thrive throughout the headwaters and the upper river, and gar dwell in the middle sections. Occasionally, largemouth bass and bluegills will be encountered, but neither species is common except in the backwaters behind the dams. For the vast majority of anglers, smallmouth bass, muskies, and flathead catfish are the species of choice with the smallmouth, of course, being the overwhelming favorite.

Let Ledges Give You the Edge

Although weather and water conditions may vary, seasons may pass, and lure choices may change, a deep water ledge remains the best place to prospect for jumbo bass on the James River and, for that matter, smallmouth rivers everywhere.

I am lucky enough to live on the banks of Catawba Creek, a Botetourt County stream filled with smallies. The flow of the James River is just a twenty-minute drive from my house, so I am able to pursue my favorite gamefish throughout the year. Even if you don't live creekside, concentrating on ledges allows you to put together year-round smallmouth bass patterns that will work whenever you go fishing.

Before delving into those patterns, it's important to understand why smallmouths are so attracted to this structure. Ledge rock—often composed of limestone—has been alternately chipped, cut, and smoothed for eons by weather and current. These forces have carved out a multitude of sanctuaries for a wide variety of aquatic insects and crayfish.

Various minnow species, sculpins, madtoms, and juvenile catfish find safe havens in the deep recesses of ledge rock. Attracted by readily-available food, smallmouths likewise find their respective niches in these stone crannies, which also serve as current breaks for bass. But the final ingredient that clinches deep water ledges as ideal bass-holding grounds is the overhead water column. A prime ledge lies in water six to fifteen feet deep, and nowhere else on a stream can smallmouths so easily prowl for food without fear of avian predators attacking from above.

Tactics for fishing ledges vary by season, so let's take a look at each season in turn.

Winter

Ledges can be productive even in cold water. On a February day after arriving home about 4:15 from teaching school, I hurried down to the creek behind my house. The stream is a small one, just twenty to thirty feet wide in most places and on average just two to three feet deep. Periodically, the creek forms ten- to fifteen-foot deep pools that possess a series of limestone ledges rising from the bottom, and I concentrated my efforts on those pools. On that cool, blustery afternoon, I landed four smallmouths before dark. The quartet had been anchored by a fine two pounder, which was lurking in the heart of the pool. This incident serves to dispel several myths about wintertime smallmouth angling. Don't believe the stories about bass "hibernating" through the winter. Their ample girth made it clear that all the bass had been feeding. Second, don't feel that you always have to use agonizingly slow retrieves to entice fish. My best fish fell for a Mepps gold Aglia spinner, retrieved rapidly. The smallie was lying in the deepest water of the pool—that is, the area equidistant from where the water enters the pool and where it begins to pick up speed as the liquid leaves the hole. The mid-pool area offers the most stable water in terms of temperature and current flow and is the winter sweet spot.

Other good cold weather offerings include Woolly Buggers, deep-diving minnow imitations and three-inch grubs on one-fourth ounce jig heads. Perhaps the premier wintertime ledge baits for big smallmouth, though, are weighted crayfish patterns and jig-and-pigs hopped slowly across the bottom. For that matter, these two crayfish imitations are great for lunker bronzebacks throughout the year.

Spring

A ledge remains a big bass magnet in the spring, but where and how you fish this structure changes significantly from the winter months. Richard Furman, who frequently fishes the James River from his home near Buchanan, looks for two different kinds of areas.

"The biggest bass hold in two places: deep water ledges that have springs or small creeks entering them, and ledges that receive full sunlight," says Furman. "In both places, the fish are merely stacking up in the warmest water, which also offers food and cover. The warmer water from the spring and small tributaries, and the water heated by the sun make both the bass and their prey more active."

One of Furman's favorite baits during the spring is a three-inch plastic crawfish rigged Texas-style, with a 1/0 hook and a one-fourth ounce bullet sinker. Although crayfish typically spend much of the winter in burrows, they become increasingly active in spring. Bogus crustaceans inched along the bottom accurately match the movements of these creatures. Furman notes that the use of a one-fourth ounce or larger bullet sinker is a key ingredient when using soft plastic in spring. Many rivers typically run high and fast during this season. If you want your plastic baits to plumb the recesses of deep water ledges, you must use enough weight for the lure to sink and stay down where big smallmouths lurk. Sometimes bullet sinkers as large as three-eighths of an ounce must be employed.

During one April excursion with Furman on the James, I watched him catch fish after fish on a variety of deep-diving crankbaits. Some of the most effective ones are the Bomber Model A series, Storm Wiggle Warts, and Luhr Jensen Hot Lips. Particularly good for trophies are six-inch black plastic lizards and larger chartreuse/white Clouser Minnows. The Clouser is a real favorite of mine; few lures or flies can so accurately mimic the flight of a panicky minnow.

Summer

Although I concentrate on ledges in the winter and spring for overgrown bronzebacks, I catch my biggest bass in summer. One blistering hot July day when local lake marinas had reported that the black bass had "shut down," I spent four hours wading a stream. Just by working ledges, I caught eight jumbo smallmouths and lost two more. My best fish was a trophy five-pound smallie. I also landed a fine three-pounder and a trio of two-pounders. During the warm weather, I prefer deep-water ledges that have riffles no farther than fifty yards above them. That inflow insures both well-oxygenated water and a constant source of food entering the area. The middle of a pool is most productive in the winter, although in summer I prefer the upper and lower ends. The most active bass will typically be holding at those points.

My favorite lures include six-inch Zoom or Mister Twister Phenom worms in pumpkinseed, black, or purple. I rig these Texas style with 1/0 hooks and one-eighth or one-fourth ounce bullet sinkers. Since the current is moderate, there is rarely any need for heavier weights. I crawl the worms through the green (i.e., deep) water between rock ledges, periodically lifting the baits a few inches or so and then allowing them to settle. Strikes usually occur on the fall or when the artificial crawler lies still.

Four-inch ringworms, in the same colors as mentioned above, also work well—especially when the fish seem to want smaller baits. The aforementioned five pounder, for instance, hit a black ringworm that was rigged Texas fashion with a size one hook and without any sinker. This leads to an important point: if you find that the fish are spooky and/or lethargic because of a summer cold front or ultra clear water, try fishing ringworms without weights. Doing so allows the bait to land gently on the surface and begin a tantalizingly slow descent. You may find, as I did, that finessing like this makes the long wait for the bait to fall worthwhile.

Dick Pickle, who operates the Wilderness Canoe Company in Natural Bridge, offers other summertime options.

"Hellgrammites, or soft plastic lookalikes, are great summertime baits," he says. "On ledge-filled streams like the upper James and New, or on streams that have lots of boulders that lie close together like the piedmont James and the Rappahannock, nothing can out fish a hellgrammite. I fish both the live and soft plastic hellgrammites the same way: very slowly above the bottom. To make them rise above the bottom, I put a splitshot some twelve to eighteen inches above the hook, causing the bait or lure to glide along."

Pickle says that topwater baits worked over ledges also draw vicious summertime strikes. Good choices include Heddon Tiny Torpedos, Rebel Pop'Rs, Zara Spook Puppies, Storm Chug Bugs, buzzbaits, and floating/diving minnows. He adds that fly-rodders should try various poppers and dragonfly or stonefly nymph imitations.

Fall

Because of the low, clear water conditions, the largest smallies are exceptionally easy to find in autumn, yet sometimes maddeningly difficult to catch. The thin water of early fall forces bass into those ledge areas that still possess deep water. Fishermen can often see bass cruising about; and just as often, the smallies will flee when an artificial makes even a gentle splat upon the water.

Don Roberts, who operates the Front Royal Canoe Company on the South Fork of the Shenandoah (800-270-8808), gives tips on how to combat this situation.

"The first thing I do is seek out ledges that have riffles or Class I rapids entering above them," he says. "The fish that gather in those ledges will be the most active, because the water there is better aerated. Second, I downsize my baits, because the smallmouths are so spooky. For example, a great fall lure is a three-inch grub on a one-eighth ounce jig head. Use light line with that bait—say six-pound test—and you will get more strikes."

I sometimes work a grub parallel to a ledge, in order to cover the entire structure. Perhaps the most effective way to fish this bait is to cast beyond the ledge, bring the grub up to the lip of the structure, and then let it tumble down into the deep water behind the ledge. Hits often take place as the grub falls. In addition to this tactic, another autumn trick for skittish smallies is to add split shot to ringworms, grubs, tube baits, and four-inch worms. Smallies will often flee as the bait enters the water and then return to smash it.

For truly balky fish and for a change of pace, try four-inch soft plastic jerk-baits such as a Shad Assassin (from Bass Assassin). Mark Frondorff, an Alexandria resident, says this is his favorite autumn artificial. He makes long casts with this soft plastic minnow jerkbait and then works it erratically back. Later in the season, Frondorff continues to probe ledges. But as the late fall rains put some color back into the water, he switches to Woolly Buggers, spinnerbaits, and jig-and-pigs.

Various flies will also produce come autumn. In fact, I believe that given the low, clear water and spooky fish, a fly-fisherman who can make accurate and delicate presentations often has the advantage over spin fishermen. Try nine-foot leaders that taper to 6X with poppers, hairbugs, and grasshoppers. Hoppers are especially effective, particularly if overgrown banks lie just upstream or adjacent to a ledge.

Overall, there is no better place to consistently take good-sized stream smallmouths than a deep water ledge. By changing just slightly where and how you fish, ledges can give you the edge over smallmouths throughout the year.

Going Soft for Smallmouths

The scene was one of the most powerful from an exceptionally memorable movie. A young Dustin Hoffman in the 1960s film *The Graduate* was cornered by a businessman at Hoffman's college graduation party. In a secretive manner, the older gentleman said that he had one word of advice that would ensure a successful future for the recent grad. "Plastics," the gent whispered to a befuddled Hoffman.

I seriously doubt that our shrewd high financier was referring to river small-mouth fishing when he uttered his magic word, but I also have no doubt that soft plastic concoctions are the premier bassing baits for today and the future.

I used to employ plastic baits for stream smallies only during cold fronts when the fish became too lethargic to chase down crankbaits or floating/diving plugs. But the more I used these soft plastic artificials, the more I became convinced that they were my best bet for catching more quality bronzebacks, regardless of fish activity levels. What's more, I learned that I didn't need a large selection of these inexpensive lures; just plastic worms, craw worms, lizards, grubs, and a few kinds of drop baits met all my stream bassing needs.

Lake largemouth fans have known for years that crawlers are a top bucket-mouth bait, but worms have been largely neglected by stream fishermen. Yet, were I restricted to just one soft plastic bait for river smallies, that artificial would be a plastic worm.

A good example of a plastic worm's effectiveness occurred on a float-fishing trip that five friends and I took several summers ago. A cold front had come through the area the day before, leaving the intense blue sky cloudless. We all knew that the fishing conditions would be tough, and as the day started my companions opted for small crankbaits or inline spinners. I chose plastic worms. Later, when we gathered for lunch, everyone had enticed some bass—except me. Of course, none of those bass had topped nine inches, and all had been caught from shallow riffle areas—the habitat for undersized fish. During the shore repast, I took quite a bit of ribbing, and several of my comrades offered me their spinners.

I said, "No thanks," and then explained what I was trying to accomplish with the worms. Because of the negative conditions, the bigger smallmouths would be in deep water haunts with vertical cover, specifically limestone ledges in eight to fifteen feet of water. My plan was to slowly drift six-inch worms through those ledge areas. After lunch, I endured another bassless hour before my pattern kicked in. First, a 14-inch mossyback fell to the worm, then a two pounder, and then, finally, what I had been hoping for. I felt a solid hit on my bogus crawler and upon setting the hook, saw a twenty-inch bronzeback break the surface. For the next five minutes, I followed the bass some seventy-five yards downstream and maneuvered it out from two different sets of ledges and one logjam before lipping my prize. The smallmouth weighed over four pounds.

That outing is illustrative for a number of reasons. First, if you become a devoted stream worm fisherman, expect your overall catch rate to go down, but also expect to catch more quality bass. The three bass that I mentioned were the only ones I caught all day; they were also the only ones over twelve inches caught during my group's trip. Second, deep water ledges are the best place to

Soft plastic baits such as this crayfish often produce fine smallmouths.

find big stream smallmouths (*see* Chapter Two). All my fish came from ledge areas, and this has been the case on a number of other excursions. Look for deep water ledges downstream from riffle or rapid areas where the current has had a chance to smooth out.

Third, although worms are a great cold front bait, don't overlook them when the fish are in an active or neutral state. On a day when the fish were aggressively feeding, I once used worms to catch six smallmouths between two and three pounds in ninety minutes, surpassing a friend who was burning a crankbait through the same pools.

Finally, keep things simple with this inexpensive bait. I use six-inch worms in pumpkinseed, purple, black, and red, rounded out with size 1/0 offset worm hooks and one-eighth through three-eighth ounce bullet sinkers, depending upon the current. The worms are rigged weedless—that is, Texas style, with the point of the hook embedded in the plastic to avoid snags.

As effective as a plain plastic worm is, a craw worm will sometimes produce better—and the latter may be best for three-pound and larger smallies. Craw worms, which are part plastic worm and part plastic crawfish, offer a larger profile than a crawler and they attract bass looking for a bigger meal. One summer day, a friend and I experienced mixed success while tossing worms most of the morning. Upon arriving at an eddy that was characterized by deep water and rocky cover, we switched to craw worms. On my first cast, a three-pound mossyback immediately sucked in the craw worm and charged upstream. While I was doing battle, my partner tossed his craw into the same section of the eddy, and he promptly had on a twin to my fish. It took me a little longer to subdue my fish than it did for my friend to land his. In fact, he had caught and released his smallie and had made another cast—on which he hooked his second three-pounder—before I finally landed mine.

What made our craw worms and that eddy such a perfect combination? Our experiences earlier that morning had shown us that the smallies were obviously not feeding actively. But we knew that if there is one creature that will turn a listless smallmouth on—particularly a jumbo smallie—it's a crayfish. Today's plastic craw worms simulate the appearance and movement of live craws better than any crankbait possibly can. And when you add the taste factor (many of today's plastic crawfish have been scent- and salt-impregnated), you truly have an imitation that is close to the real thing.

Another factor that contributed to our success was that, next to a ledge, an eddy is the best place to prospect for big smallmouths. But as is true with ledges, a very specific kind of eddy should be sought. Areas of reversing currents are common throughout many streams, but only a few present big bass potential. First, eddies must have relatively deep water; in rivers, that means areas of at least four to eight feet. Second, ignore areas that have sand or pebble bottoms. Instead, zero in on spots that feature at least basketball-sized rocks and/or submerged trees or other debris that offer places for bass to hold. When working an eddy, pay close attention to the current's direction. By its very nature, an eddy will have current flowing in different directions. Be sure to always retrieve your plastic baits with the current.

I rig craw worms Texas style and use the same size hooks and bullet sinkers as with worms. I retrieve the two baits similarly, except that I will occasionally impart a hopping motion to the craw worm and sometimes even retrieve it quite quickly—much like the way a real crawfish will react when faced with a predator. Although I use worms and craw worms for much of my soft plastic fishing, there are a trio of other baits that each have their own special applications. Chief among these is the plastic lizard. Anglers know that salamanders (or more accurately, newts) are natural enemies of spawning bass, but plastic replicas of these creatures excel at triggering strikes at any time. When lizards are retrieved rapidly across the surface, the legs of the lure start churning and smallies find the commotion hard to resist. Another way to work fake salamanders is to toss them upon a stream bank, then slowly inch them into the water. This approach can be a great tactic when you're faced with low, clear water and/or spooky bass. I was faced with those conditions one summer when a prolonged drought afflicted the area. The only way I caught mossybacks was by tossing six-inch Texas-rigged salamanders above undercut banks and then retrieving the lures so they gradually tumbled into the water.

The second member of my backup trio is the grub. Of all the plastic baits, the homely-looking grub is the most versatile. It can be retrieved slowly near the bottom like a worm, hopped across the substrate like a craw worm, skittered across the surface like a lizard, jigged up and down like a spoon, or creatively employed in any number of other ways. Three- or four-inch grubs in pumpkin-seed, motor oil, and brown can be made to mimic just about any critter that dwells in a stream. I prefer Kalin grubs because of their soft tails and life-like action. One summer day, I was working the tail end of a pool where the bottom dropped from six feet of water to nine—a place where I had caught a number of nice smallmouths in the past. On my second or third cast, a smallmouth hit the bait and set off on a searing run that eventually resulted in the grub's hook pulling free. I had one look at the fish—enough to realize that it topped four pounds. On that trip, my larger lures had failed to produce, but the three-inch grub had enticed a behemoth of a bronzeback.

My third and final backup plastic bait is a three-inch drop, or tube bait, such as the Venom Super Do. When a cold front has passed through an area, bass want something exceedingly small, and a tube bait often will work when nothing else does. Cast this lure into likely-looking areas and inch it along or leave it motionless—in effect allowing the current to give life to the bait's tentacles. A tube bait saved the day for me during one excursion when a cold front had recently slashed through the area. Until I tied on a tube, my friend and I spent a fruitless morning. During a series of six casts after the bait change, I landed two fine smallies from an eddy and experienced three additional hits—proving just how deadly this small, vulnerable-looking bait can be. Because of their diminutive size, tube baits will attract bass and panfish of all sizes, so they are not as productive as worms and craw worms for big bass. But for last-gasp situations, this artificial is unsurpassed. My favorite colors are salt-and-pepper and pumpkinseed.

I generally bring along four rods for fishing plastics. I employ a six-and-one-half-foot, medium-heavy baitcaster and a similar-length, medium-heavy spinning rod for most of my soft plastic fishing. Both of these outfits can drive home the hook in a Texas-rigged worm, craw worm, or lizard. I typically pair these rods with ten- or twelve-pound-test Trilene XT or PRADCO's Silver Thread. This relatively heavy line is useful in extracting bigger smallmouths from the rock and wood cover they inhabit. These two rods also work great for jig-and-pigs. For grubs and tubes, I prefer a six-foot medium action spinning outfit. This rod excels at casting or skipping grubs and tubes into likely areas. I spool eight-pound-test onto the spinning reels that accompany these rods. A medium action spinning outfit also works well for topwaters such as Heddon Tiny Torpedos and Rebel Pop'Rs.

For smallmouths on the James and other streams, soft plastics are the way to go. In fact, for quality river bronzebacks, I offer just one word to ensure your success: plastics!

Falling for Autumn River Bass

One of the worst myths perpetrated by outdoor writers goes something like this: "with the dipping air and water temperatures of autumn, river smallmouths go on 'feeding binges' as they attempt to put on weight for the winter, resulting in the best bass fishing of the year." Actually, this premise is misleading, for several reasons.

Bass experience feeding binges throughout the year. They always try to put on weight, and in autumn bronzebacks go through intense mood swings—resulting in some of the best and worst bass fishing of the year. To help anglers on the James and other rivers smooth out the highs and lows of autumn, here is a game plan for dealing with three major problems fishermen face at this time.

Problem One: Abnormally Low, Clear Water

After the long hot months of summer, October often brings low water of a crystalline quality to streams such as the James, New, Rappahannock, and South Fork of the Shenandoah. Barry Loupe, a Saltville resident, offers strategies that can help anglers cope with this condition.

"The most important thing I do in the fall is always use light, clear line," he says. "I'll start with eight-pound test, but if the fish aren't biting I don't hesitate to drop down to six or even four-pound test. I also recommend that fishermen not use fluorescent line, which can spook fish in clear, low water. Second, I make extremely long casts, something that lighter line will enable you to do. As you float, look for likely spots well downstream and to your right or left. A cautious approach is more important in the fall than at any other time."

Loupe adds that another good tactic is to seek out shady spots where mossybacks may hold in the transparent liquid. These could include crevices between ledges, dropoffs behind boulders, and tree-laden shorelines. Sycamores are especially common trees on Virginia's upland rivers and offer extensive root networks along partially eroded banks where bass can hide. Finally, Loupe suggests that earth tones such as pumpkinseed, black, brown, and orange work best in clear water. Try jig, plastic crawfish, or crawfish patterns in these hues. Fly-fishermen need to respond similarly. Seven-and-one-half-foot leaders probably should be replaced by nine or even 12 feet, tapering to 5X or 6X.

Problem Two: October Cold Fronts

After the relatively stable weather patterns of summer, October often brings a series of cold fronts which can play havoc with smallmouth feeding patterns. Tim Freese says that he combats this problem in several ways.

"For fall cold fronts, I follow two rules," says Freese, who hails from Arlington. "Rule number one is that I finesse, which means I fish slowly on the bottom and use natural colors—no fire tiger or hot pink, for example. Rule number two is that whatever lure I use, I strive for absolute realism in presentation. That means that I really attempt to fool the bass into hitting something that looks very natural to them."

Freese emphasizes that the way he modifies and works a grub is a perfect example of his two rules. He selects naturally-colored grubs that imitate shad, sunfish, or crawfish. Before tying a grub onto the line, he slides on a brass weight and then a red bead. Freese explains that the brass weight (the exact size depends on how fast the current is flowing) simulates a baitfish eye and the red bead mimics the gills. The guide then rigs the grub weedless on a 1/0 or 2/0 hook and tosses it below ledges. Smallmouth bass that have become lethargic because of the high blue skies and cool winds associated with cold fronts often descend into ledges. A grub crawled slowly through this structure creates the illusion of a dying creature. This bait is often too tempting for even an inactive bass to pass up. Freese adds that another outstanding lure is a deer-hair jig tipped with a soft plastic pork frog. Again, natural colors such as brown, orange, and black should be the choice for both the hair jig and the trailer—let the fish tell you which combination of hues they prefer.

Problem Three: Water Temperature Fluctuations

The third major problem that often confronts anglers in autumn is a rapid change in water temperature. Dave Roland, who operates a media production business in Reston, says he frequently encounters this condition.

"In October, Virginia often has really nice warm days, but the state also experiences cold nights when the temperature dips below freezing," says Roland. "The way I deal with this condition is to have a separate morning and afternoon fishing plan. For example, on mornings after a cold night I have found that fish congregate on the bottom along banks that have fairly deep water. So I bounce weedless grubs and weighted plastic jerk-baits along the bottom with my spinning outfit, or weighted Woolly Buggers and Muddler Minnows with my fly rod."

As the sun comes up and the water warms, Roland explains, the fish often move off the bottom and into the main channel to forage. They also become much more active and will rise to the surface to engulf minnows or various other prey. When this happens, Roland turns to surface baits such as the Heddon Tiny Torpedo and Rebel Pop'R or fly rod poppers such as the Sneaky Pete. Roland recalls several early fall days when numerous good-sized bronzebacks fell to this "hit 'em low early and hit 'em high late" gambit.

River smallmouth anglers on the James and other streams know that those supposedly classic fall days when the fish ravage every lure in sight are rare. But a game plan that takes into account the common problems we face in early fall can still make this time on the water productive.

How to Hook Panfish, Catfish, and Muskies

Although the majority of anglers who come to the James seek smallmouth bass, other fishermen are seeking panfish, catfish, or muskies. All these species are fun to catch, and I must admit that I am a great fan of the panfish clan. I especially enjoy the two species that inhabit the river in appreciable numbers: rock bass and redbreast sunfish.

Rock bass, also known as redeyes, goggle-eyes, and rock sunfish, are ounce-for-ounce some of the most aggressive fish in fresh water. In the James, redeyes typically weigh less than a half pound, but they maul a fly, lure, or live bait with great gusto and often cause a fisherman to think that a smallmouth bass has just hit his offering. Another trait of rock bass is that they come by their name honestly; they are creatures of the rocks. Any riffle or eddy with several feet of water and scattered rocks will likely host a voracious contingent of these fish. Although rock bass will frequently hit the same artificials as smallmouths do, anglers will catch more of these pint-sized battlers if they downsize their lures. For example, a standard bait for James smallmouths is a medium-sized crankbait. To focus on goggle-eyes, try an ultralight crankbait. Similarly, three-inch floating/diving minnow lures will draw smallmouths, but the ultra-light versions of hard plastic minnows will more likely attract the attention of rock bass.

Redbreast sunfish become more and more common the farther one floats downstream on the James and, like redeyes, these little gamesters infrequently top a half pound. Redbreasts, also known as yellowbelly sunfish, sun perch, sunnies, or bream (although they are not members of the perch or bream families) prefer the calmer back waters of the river. In these still pools, look for sunnies near downed trees, submerged rocks, and shoreline cuts. If I were restricted to one lure for these sunfish, I would tie on a size 2 Mepps Aglia spinner with a silver blade. Retrieve an in-line spinner rapidly past a submerged log or rock and if a sunfish is nearby, it will likely strike this lure with intensity. People who like to fly fish will find rock bass and redbreast sunfish willing partakers of their offerings. Excellent choices include grasshopper and cricket imitations and just about any nymph or terrestrial imitation in a fly box. Redeyes and sunfish are not "match the hatch" fish; in other words, you need not imitate the hatch in order to fool these gullible fish. For that reason, redeyes and sunfish make excellent "starter fish" for budding fly-fishermen.

Indeed, a beginner with any kind of fishing pole can learn the basics of angling by going after these gamefish. When my son Mark first began to fish, he and I would go to a stream and seine the shallows for bait. I would then tie on live bait such as minnows, crawfish, and hellgrammites. The rock bass and redbreasts would usually cooperate. For live-bait fishing, all you need are an inexpensive spinning outfit, six-pound test, a bobber, some sinkers, and live-bait hooks. Rock bass and redbreast sunfish deserve the piscatorial version of an Oscar as "best supporting gamefish" on the James.

An angler hoists a thirty-inch catfish caught below Arcadia.

While rock bass and sunfish rarely top a pound on the James, flathead catfish commonly break the twenty-pound barrier. One August, David Wright of Troutville and I floated the river from Arcadia to Alpine—one of the better smallmouth stretches. Wright and I were working a pool below a Class I rapid, both of us tossing crayfish imitations. Suddenly, Wright cried out that he had on a monster smallmouth; and for several minutes his rod bowed and his drag groaned. We speculated about how many pounds the smallmouth would weigh. Some five minutes into the epic battle, David and I were both convinced that he had on a state-record bronzeback. David was envisioning his picture in papers across the Old Dominion, and I was thinking that I was in on the Virginia fishing scoop of the decade. Several minutes later, though, the massive dark brown head of a creature appeared near my canoe, and both our dreams were abruptly shattered. What would have been a legendary smallmouth was just an average-sized flathead. David's fish measured thirty inches—a handsome fish to be sure—but for those who seek this game-fish it was not a wall-hanger by any means. James River anglers haul in flatheads that top thirty pounds.

While Wright fooled his catfish with a soft plastic crawfish, live baits are the choice of most anglers who fish for this species. As is true with other members of the catfish family, flatheads are omnivorous and will consume just about any creature, alive or dead. But unlike some other catfish, flatheads show a distinct preference for live critters, especially minnows and chubs. Probably the most popular bait for this square-tail catfish is a six-inch chub. Standard gear for this bait is a heavy action baitcaster, seventeen-pound test, and size one live

The James offers rapids and flat water for all levels of canoeists.

bait hooks. Flatheads generally avoid faster moving sections, preferring instead the long, deep, slow-moving pools well below rapids. These pools will likely hold more flatheads if they feature a hard bottom of pebbles or limestone. Find a hole such as this, bring along a dozen chubs, set up shop around sunset, and you should be in for a pleasant night of "catting."

Some state anglers debate whether the flathead or the muskie is the fiercest predator in the upper river, but I will not attempt to settle that argument. While the flathead is certainly a strong fighter, the muskie emanates more of a sneering, two-fisted, hardcore viciousness when hooked. And that's before you bring one into your craft; a muskie goes completely berserk when hoisted from the water. Subduing one of these toothy fish thrashing about in a canoe is like trying to stuff a mountain lion into a paper bag. It is possible, I suppose, but who would want to try?

A James River muskie—considered large—will usually top fifteen pounds, but a good many fish weighing more than twenty-five pounds are landed every year. Like flatheads, muskies frequent the slower-moving sections of the river, but this pike family member often prefers the shoreline. Look for muskies to lie on the downstream ends of water willow beds, along downed trees stretching out from the shoreline, or behind partially submerged boulders in pools. Jumbo lures are the norm for the river's muskie hunters. Magnum Bomber Long As, which weigh an ounce or more, are popular choices, as are one-ounce Cordell Red Fins. But these lures are not big enough for some anglers. I have seen homemade muskie baits that were twelve inches long—the size of a decent smallmouth. Live baits are similarly huge, and some muskie addicts will spend hours gathering carp or suckers that run eight or more inches in length. Muskie fishermen, though few in number, are some of the most serious and dedicated.

Of course, other fish dwell in the upper river. From time to time, I have caught pumpkinseed sunfish and bluegills, two other members of the panfish family. Channel catfish used to be common on the river, but the flathead is believed to have sorely decreased the numbers of its fellow catfish. Gar occur on the upper and middle sections, but they are extremely difficult to catch. Carp are found throughout the James, but very few fishermen seek out this bottom-dwelling giant that typically weighs ten to thirty pounds. In short, smallmouth bass garner the bulk of the angling attention on the river, while rock bass, redbreasts, flatheads, and muskies capture most of the rest.

Floating the James

As is true with any river, the James can be dangerous at times. Heavy rains, thunderstorms, frigid water, and a host of other conditions can afflict the canoeist, depending on the season and/or weather patterns. The first step in avoiding difficulty is to be reasonably adept at paddling a canoe.

I learned how to paddle by going with veteran canoeists who were willing to show me the basic strokes, how to size up a rapid, and how to notice potential trouble spots. Another way to learn the art of paddling is to take a continuing education course at a local high school or community college. Outdoor education programs and recreation departments regularly offer such classes. Or you can book several guided trips with one of the canoe liveries on a river.

I have found the vast majority of canoe liveries to be very safety conscious. Many will not allow a beginner on a river until that individual has viewed a safety and how-to video and received hands-on instruction at the livery. Then the individual is encouraged to make a maiden voyage with either a professional guide or someone who has at least intermediate skills.

The second step toward becoming a competent canoeist is to understand the rapids rating system. Basically, the system is as follows:

Class I: Easy, small waves; few obstructions; rescue is easy and can be accomplished individually.

Class II: Medium, clear-cut, rapids; easily-avoided obstructions; rescue is fairly easy.

Class III: Difficult, intense rapids; standing waves can swamp a canoe; boulders are scattered and can require quick maneuvering; scouting is a must; group rescue may be needed.

The author's wife casts near the put-in at Iron Gate.

Class IV: Very difficult, powerful, and potentially dangerous rapids; large canoe-swamping waves; tricky passageways among rocks; group rescue may be required.

Except for the series of intense rapids within the city of Richmond, the James is generally devoid of Class III and Class IV rapids. The one exception is the Class III to IV Balcony Falls on the Glasgow to Snowden trip, an excursion that only advanced paddlers should take. With some instruction and planning both the novice and intermediate paddler should be able to enjoy nearly all of the headwaters, upper section, and middle section of the James.

Once you have decided to enter the realm of James River canoeing, you can then go about finding your niche in this marvelous outdoor activity. To do so, you must determine what your canoeing goals are. For example, some paddlers relish the pleasure of canoeing above all else. They welcome the opportunity to venture forth on weekend excursions that may cover thirty or more miles.

Others, like myself, view the canoe as a gateway to a host of outdoor adventures. On any given trip, I will bring along a camera, fishing gear, and binoculars for bird watching. I make numerous stops in order to capture a majestic view, cast to a likely area, or identify an interesting warbler, vireo, or shorebird. And a streamside lunch is always part of the itinerary.

Family members often come with me. My son Mark likes to fish with me several times a summer while my wife Elaine feels the James is a wonderful place to relax and enjoy the beauty of nature. For paddlers like me, a five-mile journey is a good day outing, since it may take six to eight hours to accomplish. I generally opt for trips that sport nothing more than Class I to II rapids.

Other individuals just welcome the opportunity to be on the water. These recreationalists often perceive the James as a respite from the workaday world and as a place to float lazily along. They may only want to cover eight or so miles during a day (generally one mile per hour is the pace) and prefer treks either lacking in rapids or containing nothing more daunting than Class I rapids.

Fortunately, the James can satisfy the various desires of these individuals. Careful trip planning, though, is a must. Before taking any trip outside of my home Botetourt County, I call an outfitter and request current river conditions, weather reports, and recommended trips. Even though I may have floated a particular section many times in the past, I also like to ask for detailed information on the trip I eventually select. By their very nature, rivers are constantly in transition and even the most placid of sections may have changed dramatically since my last visit.

Canoe liveries can supply you with all this information and offer shuttling and rental services. I also recommend that you contact local tourism offices and have them supply information on accommodations. After my wife and I spend a day on a river, we sometimes enjoy a dinner out and a sojourn at a bed and breakfast.

Many newcomers to this pastime worry about experiencing an accident while on the river. Actually, I think this is a concern all river goers should have regardless of their skill level. The best way to avoid suffering a mishap is to learn to avoid trouble in the first place. Sooner or later, most river runners eventually will capsize. If such an event occurs, float with your feet downstream (to protect your head and chest cavity) and look for an eddy or still water to make your exit from the current. This will also be the time when you will be glad you packed a dry bag with spare clothes.

I also always wear a personal flotation device whenever I canoe. Too many people use their life jackets as seat cushions and are unprepared when danger strikes. A spare paddle, water bailer, food, sunscreen, bug spray, and first aid kit are other items you may want to pack on trips. If you encounter rapids that appear to be beyond your skills, a simple solution exists: portage around them. Although doing so is not the macho thing, it is the prudent course.

Another more subtle danger on the river is partially submerged debris, such as trees and branches, where the river current sweeps through. Often called strainers, these should always be avoided because protruding branches in the current can flip a canoe. The flow-through nature of the obstruction pins the craft under water with tons of force, even in a modest current. Steer clear of downed trees and similar structures and stay safe.

The James is the longest river in the country totally within the confines of one state. With the proper precautions, you can enjoy many pleasurable hours on a stream that is often called "Virginia's River."

Why Conservation Easements Make Sense

It is often said that experiences that happen to us when we are young shape our older lives. Such is the case with me, as two childhood events most definitely did.

When I was a 10-year-old Salem lad in 1962, my peers and I spent much time in a woodlot behind our houses. We built forts, fashioned bows and arrows (the former was a bent stick with twine, the latter a sharpened stick), unsuccessfully hunted squirrels and rabbits, and dreamed of seeing a deer—no one we knew ever had.

One day a bulldozer came through leveling our forts and the entire forest and replacing them with a housing development. I felt a bitter sense of loss.

The second came two years later. My Grandfather Willie drove me to the site of an approximately 1,000-acre Franklin County farm that had been the traditional Ingram homestead. But all that remained were subdivisions and a few woodlots—only a few acres of which an Ingram family member owned. My grandfather cried as he described the pain of losing the land, and my birthright; as I was the only Ingram male of my generation, he said, the property would have become mine.

Once again I felt that same bitterness and pledged to my grandfather that I would save money, buy land, and this time the family would possess it forever.

There were several reasons why I became an outdoor writer, but one of the main ones was that since my wife Elaine and I were both school teachers, we would never be able to afford the rural land that I so desperately wanted. So I began writing, saving as much money as possible from the income, and planning for the day when we could purchase some property.

By 1997, I had saved enough to buy our first substantial piece: a 137-acre tract (15 acres in Monroe County, West Virginia and 122 acres in Craig County) on Potts Mountain. Recalling those two earlier incidents, I began searching for a way to permanently protect the Craig land, passionately desiring two things: that the land could never become a housing development, and that my heirs (if they possessed enough wisdom not to sell the place) would always have a place where they could hunt and enjoy the outdoors. The answer was conservation easements.

Conservation easements are voluntary, permanent legal agreements between a landowner and a land trust that serves to keep rural land permanently rural. They also do the following:

- Place restrictions on a property to protect its resources and values. Those values typically include such things as hunting and fishing, timber stand improvement (TSI), and agriculture; and the resources such items as wild-life habitat, riparian zones and water quality.

- Limit certain types of uses, or prevent development from taking place. In 2006, we purchased a 120-acre tract on Sinking Creek in Craig County which has the headwater spring for that New River tributary. Wishing to protect the New River's fishery and create a stream corridor for deer and other wildlife, at least in some small way, I voluntarily created a covenant that no logging, building, or other development could ever take place in the stream's riparian zone. A few years later, we purchased an adjoining 20-acre parcel and added it to our earlier easement.

- Protect land for future generations but still permit current and future own-ers to retain many private property rights and to live on and use their land. In 2002, we bought the 150-acre tract bordering the 137-acre one on Potts Mountain. In our conservation easement, we allowed for two houses to be built on the property, one each for our children Sarah and Mark should they ever decide to live there.

- Provide landowners with potential tax benefits. By placing our two Craig County tracts under easement, the county reduced our taxes on those properties by 20%. That's because the land is now worth less monetarily to developers; but, of course, to outdoors enthusiasts the property would be worth more, as permanently protected rural lands. Landowners are also entitled to federal tax benefits, which come in the form of income tax

The author shown on his Sinking Creek land (which is under a conservation easement) in Craig County, Virginia. This headwater spring of the New River is forever protected

deductions. Since easements limit development, an appraisal is done at the time of the easement to capture the reduction in the value of the property. We have received over $80,000.00 in federal and state tax benefits.

- Prohibit future development (other than what the original landowner has decreed as allowable) even if the property is sold or passed on to heirs. If some future Ingram is foolish enough to sell our 412 acres under conservation easements, the land still cannot be developed beyond the restrictions that Elaine and I originally placed on the land. This is a great comfort to us, given my ancestors' loss of the Franklin County farm.

- Tailor the agreement to an individual landowner's needs and requests. I want to manage our easement land for wildlife and thus follow best management practices (BMP) and conduct timber stand improvement (TSI), which I have done. For example, on the Sinking Potts Mountain land, I conducted 3.6 and 6.5 acre cuts in 2004 and an 11-acre cut in 2005. On the Sinking Creek land, I conducted a 7½-acre cut in 2009 and a 7-acre cut in 2013. A major objective was to create deer bedding areas and browse, turkey nesting habitat, and early successional habitat for songbirds.

Jason McGarvey is the communications and outreach manager for the Virginia Outdoors Foundation (VOF), the state organization that holds my easements and with which I have closely worked over the years. McGarvey believes rural landowners would benefit from easements in the following ways.

- If a member is a landowner, he can place his land under easement to ensure lower taxes for his children and to ensure that his kids will always have a place to go outdoors.

- If a member hunts on leased land, an easement will ensure that the land will always remain rural and cannot be turned into a subdivision. McGarvey suggests that hunters go to landowners who lease land to them, so that these folks can learn about the tax benefits of easements.

- If landowners want to farm, timber, or make food plots on land under easement, they can continue to do all these things.

- Easements protect wildlife corridors, which are crucial for deer, turkeys, bears, and other wildlife that travels from one area to another, as well as such wildlife friendly areas as forested riparian zones and bedding areas.

- Landowners can still continue to timber, farm, and conduct other rural activities on their properties.

- Easements protect open spaces that are crucial for the future of hunting and fishing. For example, which would a hunter or angler rather have next to a property he has long hunted or fished on: a parcel that has been placed under easement, or one that has been turned into a subdivision and banned hunting and fishing?

Tom Smith is a sportsman who owns land in Grayson County and Alleghany County, North Carolina on the New River. He has placed much of his land under a conservation easement and tells why.

"We wanted to protect it from the intense development pressure which was present on that stretch of the river," says Smith. "In the 1960s and 70s, much of the land along the river in the Mouth of Wilson-Piney Creek area was sold to Appalachian Power company for the Blue Ridge Project. After the Scenic River designation stopped that project, the power company sold that land back to out of state developers, and by the early 1990s, the summer home industry was going full tilt.

"We also did it as a legal way to avoid losing the property because of estate taxes. Conservation easements are a wonderful way to manage this problem, provided, of course, you have a long term plan for the use of your property, and heirs who share that plan. Conservation easements reduce the value of the property, thereby reducing the value of the estate. There are several other tax advantages as well. I recommend that anyone interested on placing a significant amount of acreage under easement first check with a qualified estate attorney about the tax implications."

Smith emphasizes that the benefits for wildlife are tremendous as well.

"Our easement protects a lot of wildlife habitat," continues Smith. "Along the river this is especially critical, as development along the river bank can restrict wildlife travel along the river. My land will be managed as indicated by a Forest Stewardship plan, designed to manage forest for timber using best management practices which can be enforced by the land trust. In general, good, sustainable timber management is good wildlife management. This is diverse habitat, providing feeding and nesting areas for a variety of game and nongame birds, deer, small game, and non-game animals of all kinds.

"My family could have sold the land for quite a bit of money, paid the government a big chunk of it in capital gains taxes, and then been without a place to call our own. Instead, we created a situation to preserve our place in perpetuity, and make much more money in the long run by the management and sale of sustainable forest products. Each generation can sell and replant for the next. Sustainable timber production is a low overhead business that does not require daily hands on participation. It is not necessary to live on the farm and work there every day to produce timber. I hope that I have created a pretty good situation for future generations of my family."

Smith lists a number of nonprofit organizations and government agencies that can provide information and assist landowners on executing conservation easements and that have helped him with land management advice. Among those are National Committee for the New River (NCNR), the New River Land Trust (NRLT), the Blue Ridge Conservancy (BRC), the Virginia Outdoors Foundation, and the Virginia Department of Forestry (DOF).

I have worked with all of these organizations and groups except the BRC and heartily recommend them. Paul Hinlicky, a sportsman in Roanoke County, has placed his mountainside property under a conservation easement. Like Smith, he is a big fan of easements and recommends that fellow outdoors folks consider them.

"I take great pleasure in deer hunting on my land and managing it for wildlife," says Hinlicky. "And I take great pleasure in having placed 70 acres under a conservation easement and knowing that deer and other wildlife will always have this land to live on. Plus, the Virginia state tax credits that I received for the easement helped me purchase the land that was next to mine."

Hinlicky is enrolled in the WHIP program, grows switch grass stands for fawn bedding areas and for wildlife, and has conducted numerous wildlife plantings and timber stand improvement exercises on his place—all allowed by easements.

Personal Experiences

I am a huge fan of conservation easements and have many marvelous memories of hunting on our Potts Mountain and Sinking Creek properties. On the Potts Mountain parcel, I fondly recall my first deer hunt on the land in October of 1998 when I killed a mature doe on opening day of the season. Also a pleasure to recall is the time I tagged a doe on a snowy day during the late muzzleloader season in 2002. On the Sinking Creek land, my son-in-law David Reynolds killed his first deer there during the 2008 general firearms season.

To be sure, conservation easements are not for everyone. If you are the type of individual (and I emphasize that I am not criticizing this type of person) that wants to make a lot of money by selling his land to a subdivision developer, then conservation easements are not for you and would not be allowed on a parcel anyway.

But if you are the type of person who wants to permanently protect rural land, wants to set aside some land for your children to live and hunt on, likes paying lower taxes (we surely appreciate that fact every April 15), or wants the land your hunt club leases not to be developed, then conservation easements are something you should consider.

Tom Smith, an avid deer hunter for 47 of his 57 years, brilliantly sums up the essence of conservation easements.

"I believe that if you have land, love hunting, and want that tradition to continue in your family, you should seriously consider protecting your land, which can reduce estate taxes, local property taxes, and other tax burdens which can force landowners to sell," he concludes. "As we lose hunting lands, we lose hunters, and as we lose hunters, we lose an important part of the American way of life."

For more information:

- Blue Ridge Conservancy: www.BlueRidgeConservancy.org
- Blue Ridge Land Conservancy: www.BlueRidgeLandConservancy.org
- DCR Office of Land Conservation:
  www.DCR.Virginia.gov/land_conservation/index.shtml
- Land Trust Alliance: www.LandTrustAlliance.org
- National Committee for the New River: www.NCNR.org
- New River Land Trust: www.NewRiverLandTrust.org
- Valley Conservation Council: www.ValleyConservation.org
- VDACS Office of Farmland Preservation:
  www.VDACS.Virginia.gov/preservation
- Virginia Department of Forestry: www.DOF.Virginia.gov
- Virginia Outdoors Foundation: www.VirginiaOutdoorsFoundation.org

Classic Fishing Lures that Have Stood the Test of Time

If today's anglers could be transported back in time to the 1920s, they would barely recognize the way fishermen went about their pastime, especially in their use of lures. If, however, that time machine's journey stopped in the 1930s or '40s, they would be much more in tune with the art of angling.

"In the 1920s, the economy was good—it was after all, the Roaring Twenties—and fishermen seemed content to go about their sport as they had always done," said Jim Martinsen, spokesman for Mepps. "Most lures were of the 'match the hatch' variety in that they were wooden representations of baitfish and crawfish—things fish ate. However, many of these lures didn't move or act like live creatures."

Mark Fisher, director of field promotions for Rapala, agrees.

"The 1920s lures often looked anatomically correct, but their actions weren't realistic," he said. "Lures were made to look like every conceivable thing that a fish would eat, but the flash, the vibrations, the triggering mechanisms that cause a fish to hit a lure were largely lacking."

The rods, continues Martinsen, were just as clunky and stiff as the lures and usually made from metal. The Mepps' spokesman adds that his dad even fished with a telescoping metal rod, which like others of the time was a baitcaster. Line was typically a heavy, black braid.

Nevertheless, many popular lures of the '20s were outstanding fish catchers. The Creek Chub Pikie Minnow, Heddon Dowagiac Wooden Minnow, and the South Bend Bass-Oreno certainly fit into that category. The angling world and the world at large dramatically changed in the 1930s.

"The Great Depression was worldwide in the 1930s and people seemed to sense that war was imminent," Fisher said. "People weren't fishing for sport but for survival, which led to a lot of innovation."

One of those meat fishermen was Lauri Rapala, a Finnish villager. While paddling about on Lake Paijanne, he experienced an epiphany—big fish eat little fish, specifically little fish that are injured or stand out from a school in some way. And in 1936, this villager created the prototype of one the most famous lures ever—the Original Floating Rapala Minnow.

"Lauri hand carved his lure from pine bark, wrapped it in chocolate candy bar tinfoil to add flash and then melted photographic negatives for the protective coating," Fisher said. "Later, he discovered that balsa was more buoyant and stronger, so the lures became made from that.

"During the Depression while using his creation, Lauri fed his family and during World War II, he fed Finnish troops. No baitfish imitating bait before this so accurately mimicked a struggling, dying minnow."

Meanwhile in America in 1938, another artificial came onto the scene; and it too would change fishing, the Mepps Aglia spinner, created by French engineer Andre Meulnart. The Frenchman had a very different concept from others of his time—he knew that his design mirrored nothing in nature.

"The Mepps Aglia was one of the first enticer lures," Martinsen said. "Let me explain what I mean by that. If you give a cat an unlimited amount of food, eventually it will walk away. But if you throw a ball of yarn across the floor, that same full cat will chase after that yarn. The flashing of a spinner's blade has the same effect on fish as the yarn does on our fat cat.

"One of the most amazing things to me is that over 70 years later, the Aglia still accounts for over 50% of our business. When people talk about Mepps spinners, that's usually what they mean."

The 1940s saw more innovations. Martinsen relates that monofilament line and spinning rods came into existence with Mepps selling one of the first of these rods (which were guaranteed for life) for around $40, several hundred dollars in today's currency. As important as these items were, they were soon to share the angling stage with something that truly was a major leap forward.

During any major war, technological advances result and so it was with plastics. Rubber worms had existed for many decades, but they were rigid, lifeless creations that featured a texture that was not something a game fish would want to hang on to says Wayne Kent, president of the Crème Lure Company. And plastics likewise had existed in many different forms but not in any configuration that related to fishing; that is, until 1949 when Nick Crème devised an artificial lure that has become ubiquitous in bass anglers' tackle boxes—the plastic worm.

Laboring in their Akron, Ohio basement, Nick and wife Cosma combined vinyl, oils, and pigments to produce a molded plastic worm that was far superior to rubber crawlers.

"Nick Crème was a machinist by trade and he lived in the country's rubber hub where Goodyear and B.F. Goodrich had plants, so he had access to the plastic technology of the time," Kent said. "Nick often fished live nightcrawlers with a hook harness, and he knew that the rubber worms of the time moved and felt nothing like real worms. So it's not surprising that the early plastic worms he created came with a hook harness and moved more like real nightcrawlers than anything that had come before."

The Crème Wiggle Worm debuted in 1951, with a pack of five costing $1.00, and became an immediate hit with the angling public. As the demand continued to increase, Kent explains, Crème decided by the late 1950s to move his business to Tyler, Texas where largemouth bass fishing in newly made reservoirs had become the rage.

"When those lakes were created, bulldozers made pits where all the trees were piled up and where, of course, many of the bass congregated," Kent said. "That situation helped lead to some unknown individual developing a weedless worm rig, the Texas rig, which today is the most commonly used bass fishing rig."

Next, fishermen had to learn where to work that worm rig, and the Lowrance Company devised the first sonar device for fishing. And in November 1959 the company introduced a portable sonar unit that would become legendary … the Little Green Box.

By the 1960s, both the Greatest Generation and their offspring, the Baby Boomers, were on the scene and leisure fishing was once again in vogue. Then,

Marilyn Monroe, the era's paramount female sex symbol, affected, of all things, the future of fishing.

On August 5, 1962, the star-crossed legend died mysteriously, and shortly after, Life magazine featured Marilyn on its cover. Tucked away in that same issue was an article about Lauri Rapala and his balsa minnow, "A Lure Fish Can't Pass Up." That issue was Life's biggest selling issue ever, and, not surprisingly, anglers after they finished reading about Marilyn's demise turned to the article on the Rapala Minnow. Sales skyrocketed for the lure.

Mepps also came out with another classic lure that decade, the Mepps Black Fury. The lure came with squirrel hair on the treble hook, and with the offer that youngsters could turn in squirrel tails for lures or money. The news about the Black Fury and the tail offer swept through the elementary school that I attended at the time, many of my peers boasting that they could buy untold numbers of lures with the money earned from turning in gray squirrel tails.

In 1967, another classic lure came into existence—the initial "alphabet" crankbait. But first, some historical perspective. Perhaps the largest hard plastic fishing company in the United States is Arkansas' PRADCO, which over the

The Rebel Pop-R is a classic river smallmouth lure.

decades purchased many of the small companies that contributed to the development of various categories of artificials. Among the companies that PRADCO now owns (and their classic lures and year of origin) are Heddon (Tiny Torpedo 1954, Zara Spook 1939), Lazy Ike (1938), Arbogast (Jitterbug 1920s), Bomber (Model A 1988), plus Smithwick, Rebel, and Cordell among others.

"Heddon had manufactured a precursor to the modern day crankbait in the 1920s, the Vamp," said Lawrence Taylor, public relations director for PRADCO. "The Vamp had a lip to take the lure down and it gave off vibrations similar to today's crankbaits."

But Taylor says that a quantum leap forward occurred in 1967. That's when Fred Young of Tennessee carved the initial Big O from a block of balsa wood and named the artificial after his brother Odis. Soon, though, Cordell transferred the design to hard plastic, which proved to be a wise business move as the crankbait sold 1,300,000 baits its first year on the market and helped spawn the upsurge in crankbait use which continues today.

In the 1970s, another lure burst into prominence; one with a so simple and basic difference, in fact, that it is a surprise that no one had thought of it before.

"The year 1972 was when Mister Twister came up with the idea for the Curly Tail Grub," Martinsen said. "The company also came out with its Phenom Worms, which likewise have a Curly Tail and have been much imitated."

The 1980s saw many lure companies expand their offerings and also proved how quickly many artificials fall in and out of popularity, with only a few becoming true classics. Three baits in particular stand out as examples, one of which was the Knight Lit'l Fishie (basically a soft plastic minnow impaled on a jig hook), which was introduced in 1980. During the early 1980s, I remember fishing Virginia's just-opened Lake Moomaw, and everyone, it seemed, was employing this bait for bass. I have not seen anyone tie on this bait for many years.

"The Lit'l Fishie is a perfect example of a lure that still catches fish but no one talks about anymore," Wayne Kent said. "This bait is so simple to fish—all you do is cast it out and retrieve it a moderate speed—that anybody can catch fish with it."

A second lure, the Rebel Pop-R actually came out in either 1977 or 1978, but quickly disappeared from the company's catalog and sporting goods stores' shelves. But then a magazine article appeared in the early 1980s labeling the Pop-R as the secret bait of the bass pros, a frenzied demand for this surface chugger occurred, and the lure has remained a big seller ever since. Indeed, the Rebel Pop-R now is generally considered a classic lure.

The third member of our trio is the Rapala Shad Rap, which originated in 1982.

> "The distinct, tight wobble of the Shad Rap makes it an appealing bait for a variety of game fish," Fisher said. "When the Shad Rap first came out, sales were so good and the lure was so hard to find, that some people were renting them by the hour. I think one of the reasons for its continued success is that its movement and profile, and its back and belly flash, can imitate a shad or herring, which are found in so many waters."

One more lure from the 1980s bears mentioning, the Lunker City Slug-Go. As I recall, I met the lure's inventor, Herb Reed, at the 1987 Bassmasters Classic. Reed enthusiastically told me about a new type of lure that he had created (a soft plastic jerkbait) that to me looked like an elongated chunk of lifeless plastic. I silently dismissed the lure as not even worthy of a temporary fad and moved on to the next booth.

By the time of the next Classic, however, fishing the Slug-Go had become an obsession for bass anglers, and I had an assignment from a national magazine to profile Reed and his creation. Today, nearly every soft plastic company makes a jerkbait.

> "The Slug-Go and other soft plastic jerkbaits are perfect examples of lures that don't look like anything alive when they are inside a plastic bag, but come alive in the water," Fisher said. "In that sense, they are the opposite of 1920s baits, which looked like fish prey but didn't act like something alive."

Another soft plastic jerkbait sensation debuted in 1996, the Yamamoto Senko.

> "Gary Yamamoto wanted to design a jerkbait that had a different action than the other ones that had come on the market," said Ron Colby, operations manager for the company. "But everything he came up with seemed to be too fat or too long.

> "Finally, Gary hit upon the idea that he wanted to develop something that looked exactly like those yellow 5-inch Bic ballpoint pens and so the Senko was

born. The tip of its tail is like the ballpoint end, and the head of the Senko and the body are the same diameter as the pen. Rigged on a Wacky Rig, the Senko undulates, curls up, and falls erratically, just like a leaf blown about like the wind."

What will become the classic lures from the early years of this century and beyond?

"Faddish lures from the 20th Century included baits that glowed in the dark and others that were motorized and they all failed," said Jim Martinsen. "Perhaps some future 21st Century classic lure might be one that is holographic and moves in some unique way."

Mark Fisher votes for the X-Rap, another minnow imitation from Rapala. Lawrence Taylor believes that one of the subsurface walk-the-dog style plugs may emerge as a classic, or perhaps the Chatterbait, which is a hybrid spinner-bait, crankbait, and jig.

Whatever happens, we are not likely to return to the days of the 1920s when a game animal was used to catch a sport fish.

"Old timers back then would float a board that had a squirrel with a hook harness on top," Fisher said. "When those fishermen felt that the board had floated out to where these huge northern pike were holding, they would jerk the board out from under the squirrel and let it swim about. Those guys caught some huge pike with that tactic."

- Crème… www.CremeLure.com
- Mepps… www.Mepps.com
- PRADCO… www.LureNet.com
- Rapala… www.Rapala.com
- Yamamoto Custom Baits… www.Baits.com

The Marvelous Maury River:
The Upper James River's Main Tributary

The Maury River is the Upper James River's largest and most important tributary from both a fishing and paddling perspective. I have paddled the entire length of the river from Rockbridge Baths to where it enters the James at Snowden. Here's how you can do the same.

Overview

John Mays, who is part owner of Twin River Outfitters (TRO) in Buchanan, maintains that the Maury River is definitely a spring and early summer run. The waterway is normally only available from April through June 15, depending on rainfall in the area. Mays considers the Maury runnable between 1.5 feet (minimum level) to 4.5 feet (maximum safe level) on the Buena Vista river gauge. Information on gauges can be found in the appendix. The ideal level seems to be between 2.0 and 3.0 feet, confirms Mays. But during that window of opportunity, the fishing and aesthetics can both be quite special.

"The scenery on the Maury River is impressive," said Mays. "The landscapes visible from the river are typically farm lands or woods with only a few houses visible along the way, and those houses are around Lexington. The average width of the Maury varies greatly but is frequently less than 50 feet across with runnable river channels only a few feet wide.

"Unlike the James River where you can look down river a half mile, the Maury is much smaller and narrower with many turns along the way, frequently letting paddlers only see a few hundred feet ahead. Paddlers will see many stone works remaining from the old canal system [James River and Kanawha Canal] that operated in the 1800s as it made its way up the Maury River to Lexington."

Mays says that commercially TRO runs two different sections of the Maury River. Because of the intense whitewater in the Goshen Pass area where Class IV+ rapids punctuate the stream, the livery doesn't offer any trips there. TRO has found the following two sections, or variations of them, to be what the majority of clients wish to paddle when they float the stream.

The first section, says Mays, is the 6 miles from East Lexington at Jordan's Point Park on river right to the Route 60 take out (Ben Salem Wayside) on river right above Buena Vista. The outfitter describes the East Lexington excursion as "a fun trip with a few interesting rapids," as several Class IIs dot the stream. The Chessie Nature Trail runs along river left for the majority of this section. Float fishermen can make this trip three miles longer by putting in at Bean's Bottom, but then they will have to do a 200-yard portage around the Jordan's Point Dam.

The second, continues the outfitter, is from Glen Maury Park on river right in Buena Vista to Glasgow at Locher Landing on river right, which is a 12-miler. This trip contains over ten Class I to II rapids, making it a good choice for people with intermediate paddling skills, emphasizes Mays.

"Folks can also paddle the 13.5 miles from Rockbridge Baths to Beans Bottom," he says. "We don't run this trip commercially due to the difficulty, as it is a very challenging one and should only be run by strong intermediate level paddlers.

"The Rockbridge Baths float features tons of challenging Class II rapids and some impressive river cliffs along the way. You will need to have at least 2.0 feet on the Buena Vista gauge to run this section or you will be getting out of your boat a lot. The Goshen Pass run is for experts only and contains Class III and IV rapids and is runnable in the winter or after significant rain events. Goshen Pass is so difficult that no commercial liveries run this section."

I need to add a few relevant points to this trip lineup. I agree with Mays about the hazards of the Goshen Pass area. On several occasions I have wade fished this area, but the pass is no place, especially in the spring, for float fishermen in a canoe or johnboat.

The Rockbridge Baths to Alone Mills (8 miles) float, which is the next one downstream from Goshen, is one of the most scenic in the Old Dominion, with its soaring cliffs, heavily forested mountainsides, and mid-river boulders. However, as Mays notes, so many major rapids exist that float fishermen may well have to spend more time portaging than fishing. I have caught some very nice smallmouths on the Rockbridge Baths float, but I have also spent a great deal of time portaging. The put-in is on river right off Route 602 below the Route 39 Bridge, and the take-out is on river left below the Route 622 Bridge. This access point is on private land and traditionally the land owner has allowed access. Please be courteous and ask for permission to access the river here.

The Alone Mills to Beans Bottom (5½ miles) junket does not flaunt as many rapids as its predecessor, but some Class I and II rapids do pock this section, and the latter can be especially challenging in the spring. The take-out is on river left near the Route 631 Bridge. The next float, the Bean's Bottom one, is just 2½ miles long, and the last part of it is in the slow water above the dam at East Lexington.

The East Lexington to Ben Salem Wayside getaway is one I have taken numerous times. The remains of two dams create some Class I to II rapids, but the average paddler should be able to satisfactorily negotiate these rapids during normal flow conditions. Keep in mind, though, that the Maury's Class II rapids can metamorphose into technical and dangerous Class IIIs in the spring. Guide Jarod Harker of Confluence Outfitters says that this is one of the best floats on the entire Maury and has the potential to produce 16- to 20-inch smallies, especially in April and May. Harker adds that the Maury as a whole is a very underrated smallmouth waterway and well worth a look from fans of the James.

Twin River Outfitters guide Richard Furman describes the Maury "as a smaller version of the James with similar rock and wood cover and an abundance of water willow beds." Both guides maintain that the same lures and flies that perform well on one river will do well on the other.

Float fishermen should note that they can extend the East Lexington getaway by 1½ miles, should they choose to paddle to the Route 60 Bridge. A river left take-out exists there via Route 608. Paddlers should also be aware that they can not put in at this access point and make a "through" trip and take out at Glen Maury Park downstream. Moomaw's Dam, a stone edifice that is 20 feet high, lies in between and is privately owned. Portaging around this dam on private land is not allowed.

The Glen Maury Park to Glasgow trip features more dam remains and Class I and II rapids. Obviously at 12 miles in length, the Glen Maury float is one where anglers will have to fish at a faster clip, making it ideal for run and gun-style fishermen. This junket features a wide variety of habitats to probe: water willow beds, sycamore root wads, bank eddies, deep water ledges, and current breaks in the form of boulders.

Also of note is that there has been much discussion in recent years about the removal of the dam at East Lexington. The structure is a menace to navigation and a danger to both swimmers and fishermen. The dam serves no purpose and hopefully will be eliminated.

I often have said and written that the Maury is the second most beautiful river in the Old Dominion, behind only the Rappahannock. The East Lexington float merely reinforces this opinion. Within the first two miles, you'll drift by towering cliffs on river left, heavily wooded hillsides, and a Class I–II rapid.

At the two-mile point, you will come to Emore's Dam and the Class I that is created. This is a good place to stop for a shore lunch. Next comes Chittum's Island (take the right channel for ease of paddling) and then you will pass under the Interstate 81 Bridge.

The Maury is one of the most beautiful rivers in the Southeast.

Following on the itinerary is the remains of the South River Dam and a Class II rapid; the safest path is usually down the middle. The South River itself, entering on river left, soon after mingles with the Maury. On one trip with friend Doak Harbison, he caught two 16-inch smallies, which fell to a broken back Rapala, in this area. Doak employs this lure on some 80 percent of the casts he makes, believing it can attract bass both as a surface bait and as one retrieved below the surface.

After the South River enters, you will pass by two islands and then enter a long straight stretch with scattered riffles. For most of the rest of the trip, scattered riffles are the only examples of swift water, except for a lone, easy-to-navigate Class I rapid. The sound of traffic will soon clue you to the fact that Route 60 is running alongside river right and that the Ben Salem Wayside is not far away.

The Maury River did not receive its current appellation until 1945 when the Virginia General Assembly renamed the North River. Matthew Fontaine Maury is the stream's namesake as he was crucial to the South's efforts in the Civil War. Known as the "Pathfinder of the Seas," Maury was an expert at charting ocean currents and winds. Later, he served the Confederacy as its chief of seacoast, river, and harbor defenses. Because of Maury's love for the North River and its beauty, his last request was for his body to be transported through the Goshen Pass on its way to a final resting place in Richmond.

Today, modern river runners can understand what Matthew Maury knew some 150 years ago—the Maury River is a pearl of great price and well worth a visit.

Trip Planner

For canoe rental and shuttles, contact:

- Twin River Outfitters: (540) 261-7334 or www.CanoeVirginia.net.
- Confluence Outfitters: (434) 941-9550 or www.ConfluenceOutfittersVA.com

The Virginia Canals & Navigations Society is an organization created to preserve and enhance the heritage of our inland waterways and educate the public about such historical events as the canal era of the 1800s. The organization is also heavily involved with creating river atlases, such as *The Maury River Atlas*. I used the atlas to help me write this chapter. With the help of the book, I have paddled the entire Maury except, of course, for the Goshen Pass whitewater.

For more information: www.VAcanals.org.

The Headwaters

1 Iron Gate to Gala 48

2 Gala to Eagle Rock 57

3 Eagle Rock to Narrow Passage 62

4 Narrow Passage to Springwood 70

5 Springwood to Buchanan 75

6 Buchanan to Arcadia 80

7 Arcadia to Alpine 84

8 Alpine to Glasgow 89

9 Glasgow to Snowden 94

1

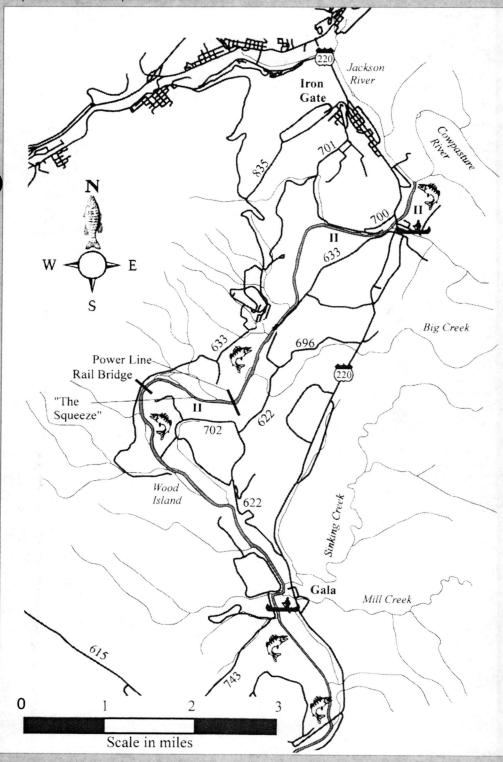

1 Iron Gate to Gala

TRIP: Iron Gate to Gala in Botetourt County

USGS QUADS: Clifton Forge and Eagle Rock

DISTANCE: Nine miles

MAP: Opposite, page 48

RAPIDS: Three Class II rapids, several Class Is and riffle areas

ACCESS: South of Iron Gate beneath Route 220 Bridge. Put-in is on river left. Steep gravel road leads to put-in. A few places to park exist. Take-out is on river left and up Sinking Creek where it enters the James at the Gala Gas Plant. Parking is available in a gravel lot.

The James River comes into existence near the community of Iron Gate, where the Jackson and Cowpasture rivers commingle. Their merging produces an eddy—that is, an area where the current "reverses" or forms a mini-whirlpool. I have spent many pleasant hours wading that eddy in search of fish. It is both amazing and humbling to consider that the small pool of water beneath me transforms into a mighty waterway that eventually empties into Chesapeake Bay. Historically, it is also humbling to contemplate that this eddy is part of the same river where John Smith, Pocahontas, and the early settlers of Jamestown played out the events that began this nation's history.

I love all aspects of a river—the fishing, canoeing, bird watching, and overall nature study—so I always have my eyes open. Near the eddy, I once witnessed one of the most aggressive acts of animal behavior I have ever seen. The belligerence took place across from the eddy on river left, in a water willow patch. Water willow—commonly (yet mistakenly) known as pickerel grass or river grass—is truly an integral part of the food web on the James and other rivers in the Southeast. Water willow is not a willow at all but a form of aquatic grass that thrives in the transition zone between shore and stream. This green plant usually grows no taller than 15 to 18 inches, but, where it exists, both terrestrial and aquatic life meet to mate, munch, and meander.

One steamy July morning, I noticed an unusual amount of surface commotion adjacent to that weed bed. Wading over to it, I observed hordes of smallmouth bass feeding around the water willow. Damsel flies were emerging and attempting to fly for the first time. Some of the luckier creatures had escaped from the surface film and now desperately clung to the vegetation itself. This had not stopped the onslaught of the bass, however, which were almost beside themselves as they swam furiously among the water willow stems in an attempt to attack the "damsels in distress." Other bass constantly churned the surface as they gulped damsel fly after damsel fly.

At that moment, I would have given just about anything to have had a fly rod and a damsel fly imitation in my possession to hurl in the general direction of the rampaging bass. But even without it, a strike was unavoidable. In the next 45 minutes I caught a number of smallies on various topwater lures. Then, as suddenly as the feeding frenzy began, it ended. Once again, temporary calm reigned in the tempestuous world of the river.

Continuing downstream, a rock bluff soon appears on river left, followed by a moderate Class II rapid. The best path through the rapid is on far river right. Taking that route will enable the paddler to avoid the most intense part of the rapid. I have enjoyed excellent surface action above the rapid, and fair fishing below it. At one time, the Route 220 Bridge was located here, making it a popular place to access the James. During the summer, many anglers would gain access to the river at the bridge and then wade upstream to the eddy at the head of the James. The river is too high to wade this section in spring.

The state, however, removed the old bridge and replaced it with the bridge listed earlier in The Essentials section of this chapter. Few people now fish the mile or so upriver from the current structure; they are blocked by the Class II rapid as well as their desire to travel downstream.

At the present Route 220 Bridge below Iron Gate, river visitors will find a point of land on river left that campers use. Below that point, where the James makes a small outside bend, is some outstanding rock and wood cover on river left. This is an excellent place to work plastic worms, jigs, streamers, and crayfish imitations. I have landed several nice bass here.

For much of the rest of this trip, the water carries you along at a quick clip. The excursion typically takes about 10 hours to fish given the high quality of the habitat. Of course for the canoeist, this trip will take less than five hours. Generally, I allot about an hour per mile for fishing purposes while folks floating can cover two to three miles per hour depending on current and how much they want to partake of other activities such as birding and photography.

After a short straight stretch that offers little midstream cover and poor fishing, you'll see a tiny island. Approximately 50 yards in length and just 50 or

The Iron Gate float is very isolated and the fishing is sublime.

so feet wide, this island is not a major fish-holding structure. Canoeists can take either the left or right channel around the island, but passage is usually better on the left side.

Several hundred yards past the island, the second major rapid for the James comes into view. The best passage is left of center for this Class II. This is a rapid that is most easily run in the spring, when water levels are high. By summer, the rapid often flaunts a number of partially submerged rocks—particularly on the far left side—that can make for a bumpy ride. When water levels are low, it's often easier to exit the canoe and walk through the rocks on the far left.

Next, a long outside bend on river right comes into sight. This portion of the Iron Gate jaunt probably provides the best opportunity for anglers to duel with a nice smallmouth. To understand why, one has to realize the importance of outside bends on the James. Some rivers, the New for example, gain their bass fishing potential by their rapid/pool constitution. Although the James hosts many rapids, the major fish-holding features on the stream are its numerous outside bends. Whereas inside bends are typically shallow and characterized by pebble-sized rocks and lack of wood cover, outside bends feature water depths between 4 and 15 feet, an abundance of downed trees and limbs, and good-sized boulders and ledges that run out from the shoreline.

Sycamores, silver maples, and ironwood commonly thrive along outside bends of the James, but it is the sycamores that present the best cover. These tall, stately trees (which have brown bark that constantly flakes off and falls into the river) form leafy canopies that provide cooler water and ambush points for fish in the summer. Throughout the year, the root systems of sycamores (because of natural erosion) extend out from the bank and provide niches where bass wait for prey to blunder by. Indeed, some days on the James I concentrate mainly on fishing these sycamore "root wads." During any fishing trip on the Iron Gate float, I recommend that anglers spend a great deal of time on this outside bend—the first major one on the James.

The next prominent feature is a mild Class I rapid. Passageways are numerous and present no difficulties. Above this rapid some fairly deep water exists and is a good place to work crankbaits or Clouser minnows in the spring, and soft plastic jerkbaits during the summer months. Below the rapid lies a fairly shallow eddy on river left. Catfish anglers frequent this eddy and some nice flatheads have come from here. Because of a lack of wood and rock cover, however, smallmouths don't linger here—and neither should bass fishermen.

Next, anglers should be able to glimpse Route 633 through the trees on river left. Fishing opportunities are limited in this fairly shallow, straight stretch, where mostly smaller bass dwell. A "rolling riffle" with several foot-high waves comes next, but this riffle is not at all difficult to paddle. The Route 633 Bridge at Glen Wilton is within sight now as well.

Glen Wilton is an extremely charming village that features country houses, well-manicured lawns, and vegetable gardens seemingly behind every home. The first time I paddled this section, I spent some time with several local people who were very willing to offer tips about floating through the area—typical of the outgoing nature of Glen Wilton's inhabitants.

Below the bridge, some very shallow water with little fish-holding cover exists for over a hundred yards, and I quickly paddle through here. Within sight of the bridge, an easy Class I rapid appears; run it right through the center. Quickly maneuver your canoe to river right and work a several hundred-yard shoreline that features some prime smallmouth habitat: overhanging sycamores with their complex root structures, undercut banks with lots of niches for game-fish, and some fallen trees with a multitude of horizontal cover. This is a great bank at which to toss a jig-and-pig—a good lure choice from spring through fall.

Next you will come to another Class I rapid and a mid-river island— the first fair-sized one on the upper James. Islands are marvelous fish attractors, especially when they create eddies, provide areas for water willow, and produce downstream points—all features of this island. Run to the left of the island (the right side is too shallow, especially in the summer and fall). Fly-fishermen will find the pockets along the island delightful places to drop nymphs and streamers in as they course by. Spin fishermen should cast buzzbaits and grubs to those same areas. Please be sure to look for partially submerged rocks during your downstream progress. I have caught several fine smallmouths from this section, but I always keep watch for potential hazards.

The next major feature is an outside bend on river left that features a number of downed trees and deep water. A power line across the river helps mark the area. My wife Elaine and I have caught some solid smallmouths from this bend, but it is not as good as many others on the river. The bottom that extends out from the bend is mostly sand and muck—offering little cover for fish or the creatures they feed upon. After a few casts to the log jams, continue downstream.

The following long, shallow straight stretch offers boring paddling and poor fishing. This section, which is really nothing more than a shallow riffle, does afford a few patches of water willow, but they border water too shallow to provide ambush points or safe havens for fish. The next section, however, is anything but mundane. Known locally as "The Narrows" or "The Squeeze," the Class II that rears its dastardly form on river left is one of the most treacherous rapids on the entire James. The problem, I suppose, is one of physics. The terrain of this area forces the James to rush through a narrow channel of no more than 15 yards in width, making "The Narrows" the most confined part of the entire river. All of the water is forced through a very constricted area, which just happens to include a number of submerged boulders that create standing waves several feet high. Adding to the danger of this rapid, the current forces boaters to the left where a rock wall and overhanging tree limbs stand guard, waiting to cause all kinds of havoc for canoeists.

A number of years ago in the month of June, I passed through The Narrows for the first time. Several other paddlers and I watched a father and son team go through the rapid first, be belted about by the standing waves, lose control of their craft, and promptly overturn, losing all their gear. They were forced to abandon the river and walk to a nearby farm for help. Thankfully no one was injured, but their day on the river was ruined. As bad as that accident was, at least the current didn't slam them into the rock wall, which is always a possibility.

My second trip through this rapid was my last. My companion, Fred Cramer of Roanoke, wanted to attempt it and we, too, immediately encountered difficulty. The standing waves flipped the boat around backwards, but—miraculously—we were able to bumble our way through the rapid without tipping over. We were not able to turn our craft around until the rapid ended, some 50 yards downstream.

Other horror stories abound. A student of mine (I am a high school English teacher in Botetourt County) sank his johnboat while attempting to navigate this rapid one March. This leads to two suggestions: First, because of "The Narrows," boaters should not attempt the Glen Wilton trip during cold or high water conditions. My student experienced the early stages of hypothermia—a potentially deadly affliction—from the icy water. Second, only expert paddlers should attempt this rapid. As mentioned earlier, I no longer run "The

Narrows." There is a calm backwater on river right above it, and you will find it is simpler to debark here and pull your boat across the shallow gravel bar on that side. My wife and I recently gave that advice to a pair of novice paddlers we met right above "The Narrows." They were floating this section for the first time. I told them not to run the rapid, but they decided to do so anyway—and quickly sank their canoe. Be forewarned.

After "The Narrows," a railroad bridge appears several hundred yards downstream. In that area, water willow thrives in great abundance on several sand bars and offers the potential to catch a musky. These toothy monsters sometimes grow over three feet long on the James, and from their lairs in water willow beds often terrorize baitfish and small carp. One summer I caught a 26-inch chain pickerel (like the musky, a member of the pike family) from those beds—the largest chain I have ever landed.

Next, a long outside bend on river right comes into view. This outside bend, which borders farm land and fields, offers perhaps the best smallmouth bass fishing on this entire section. Three springs and one branch enter this bend, providing warmer water in the spring and cooler water in the summer and fall, making them fish magnets throughout the fishing season. This section also contains exceptional rocky cover. Basketball-sized and bigger rocks extend from the shoreline and a number of hardwoods have tumbled into the water over the decades. Any time rock and wood cover like this exists, jumbo-sized smallmouths flourish, and I have caught and released a number from this bend. In fact, this bend is so productive that I usually fish it twice. After the initial pass, I paddle upstream and work it again. A good approach is to toss grasshopper imitations, topwaters and soft plastics toward the bank on your first run through. Then, on the second, employ deep-running crayfish crankbaits and minnow-imitation stickbaits and streamers across the submerged rock and wood. A point extending from river right ends this bend and a shallow riffle area follows. A very unremarkable Class I then comes into view; probably the best channel is left of center, but this rapid should present few challenges. Cast grubs and streamers into the pocket water behind partially submerged boulders in midstream.

Next is the approximately one mile long Woods Island. Take the left channel for the deepest water. I often see great blue herons, green herons, and belted kingfishers along the island; songbirds such as orioles, vireos, and numerous warblers dwell on the left bank during spring and summer. I like to identify the species of these birds by listening to their songs and hopefully introduce my boatmates to the marvelous world of birds as we drift by. The James, like most Virginia rivers, is a bird watchers' paradise.

After the island ends and the James "rejoins," a sycamore-shrouded bank looms and offers some fishing opportunities. The river moves through here relatively fast, so use lures such as buzzbaits, grubs, and streamers that can be quickly retrieved. Soon after that bank, you will see the most beautiful part of the Iron Gate excursion: a massive rock bluff that overlooks a deep pool on river right. On one of my trips through here, I simply had to stop on the gravel bank across from the bluff and take some pictures of this stunning sight. On river left, directly downstream from the bluff, some wall remains of the Kanawha Canal can be found. Generally, wherever remnants of the canal remain, good fishing also is a given, and the rule holds true here.

The Kanawha Canal reached this area of the James in the mid 1800s and over the decades remnants of its rock walls gradually crumbled into the river. The intention of the canal—the inspiration of the James River and Kanawha Company—was to link the James and Kanawha rivers by means of a canal, dam, and road system. Water commerce was supposed to flourish, especially the shipping of tobacco. Although the idea of canal transport did not survive the advent of the railroad, the ruins of the system add beauty, historical charm, and fish cover to the James.

When you leave the remnants of the canal behind, you also leave the best fishing of this section. All that remains are two long, straight stretches, each several hundred yards long, punctuated by a riffle. Both sections contain fair cover on river left in the form of overhanging sycamores and dropoffs along the shoreline. The two sections also host scattered water willow beds on river right. These beds typically hold bass only early and late in the day when they move in to feed on minnows and small terrestrial creatures that have made the fatal error of falling into the water.

Take-out is on river left by means of Sinking Creek where it enters. Several hundred yards above the Columbia Gas Company you will hear the sounds of its engines. Within a hundred yards you can smell the gassy emissions. To debark, you will have to paddle up Sinking Creek for a minute or so. There is plenty of parking in a gravel lot.

2 Gala to Eagle Rock

TRIP: Gala to Eagle Rock in Botetourt County

USGS QUADS: Eagle Rock

DISTANCE: Four miles

MAP: Page 58

RAPIDS: One Class I, numerous riffle areas

ACCESS: At Gala, the put-in is where Sinking Creek enters the James at the Gala Gas Plant on Route 220. Parking is available in a gravel lot. You will paddle down the creek a brief while to reach the James. At Eagle Rock via Route 683 just off Route 220, lies the access point. Paddle up Craigs Creek for a few yards and then haul your boat up a short, steep dirt incline to reach the gravel parking lot.

The Gala to Eagle Rock jaunt is yet another brief afternoon trip on the upper James. This four-miler usually takes no more than five hours to float fish and offers good fishing for smallmouth bass. Canoeists, however, may take only two hours or so to pleasantly drift through here, and may want to combine this float with the Iron Gate to Gala stretch. The overall lack of deep water and outside bends keeps this section from being an angler destination for big bass. Nevertheless, plenty of good areas exist. The first is at the put-in behind the Columbia Gas Company. Immediately on river left is a rock bluff followed by a shoreline pocket that is lined with a number of downed trees. An expansive water willow bed lies across from the bluff.

On one July morning before sunrise, I caught a 20-inch smallmouth from that grass bed on a soft plastic jerkbait. Dahlberg Bass Divers work well here, too. The early morning and late evening hours often find bronzebacks cruising this vegetation, but the sun angle prevents fish from being here during most of the daylight period. Some good deep-water cover exists between the bluff and bed.

A riffle sends you away from the put-in area and some very fine bass habitat immediately comes into view. As you drift through the riffle, cast streamers and grubs to a combination grass bed and backwater to your left and an undercut bank to the right. The riffle clips along at a good pace, and I'm always in a quandary as to which direction to cast and yet maintain control of the canoe. A good solution is to let one canoe partner fish the first half of this 100-yard stretch and the other the second half.

2

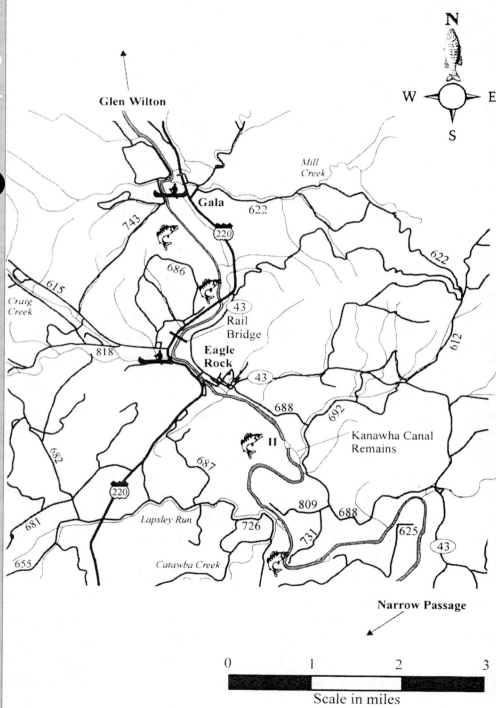

Glen Wilton

Mill Creek

Gala

622

622

743

686

622

615

Craig Creek

43

Rail Bridge

818

Eagle Rock

612

43

688

692

Kanawha Canal Remains

682

II

687

220

809

688

681

Lapsley Run

726

731

625

43

655

Catawba Creek

Narrow Passage

N

W   E

S

0   1   2   3

Scale in miles

A ledge/riffle follows. There is limited fishing potential along this section and the ensuing 100 yards or so. Catfish anglers often spend the night on river right and the smoldering remains of their campfires add pungency to the air on a morning float. Downstream, a series of ledges, dropoffs, and pools dominate the right side of the river. A good game plan for this area is to paddle down the far left side of the river so as not to spook the fish, then maneuver up to a ledge and hold the boat right below the limestone formation. Most of the ledges are in shallow enough water to stand on while casting into the pool upstream. In the summer, you can even rest the bow of your canoe on the ledges and use them as anchor points.

Once this series of ledges concludes, a "false" eddy on river right emerges. I have seen a number of float fishermen spend too much time in this type of place, lured by the erroneous belief that any kind of eddy holds gamefish. I must admit that on my initial Gala trip, I too was deceived by the outer appearance of this eddy. It has good water depth and the upstream current does channel into the area. But it is almost totally lacking in wood and rock cover, and even worse, the eddy possesses a mud bottom. A farmer's cows often muck about in the vicinity, adding to the area's undesirability. Eddies can be superlative small-mouth sanctuaries, but they must host some kind of rock and/or wood cover and depths of at least four feet to consistently attract fish. Don't waste time casting into this one.

After the false eddy, paddle to the left bank and explore some excellent shoreline cover. I have caught a number of two-pound smallies from this bank. One of my most consistent techniques from spring through fall here is to work four-inch ringworms in pumpkin-pepper, black, and purple along this bank. Deep water patterns such as Shenk's Black Sculpin and Murray's Madtom will dredge up big smallmouths, too. Target any downed trees, sycamore root wads, or undercut banks.

At the terminus of this bank, the river takes a short, quick swing to the right as you pass through a riffle. Shortly downstream, you will glimpse the Route 220 Bridge above Eagle Rock. That bridge signals some more excellent fishing as well as a Class I rapid—the only rapid of any consequence on this float. That excellent fishing occurs in a narrow eddy on river left. I paddle to the far right of the eddy and then enter from the downstream end of it. With the reversing currents of the eddy keeping the canoe "trapped" inside, I like to

Mark Ingram portaging "The Squeeze," also known as "The Narrows." On any trip on the James, please consider portaging if the rapid appears daunting.

probe this area for upwards of 30 minutes. Sometimes, the smallmouths may want a Texas-rigged plastic worm dragged across the bottom, at times they make take a crankbait bumped across the rocks, and on other occasions I have done well "swishing" Tiny Torpedos across the surface. This is also great water to toss a favorite smallmouth bass fly: the improved sofa pillow. Skate the sofa pillow in short bursts just under the surface—and hang on! Below the eddy, the Class I rapid appears directly under the Route 220 Bridge. Channels are numerous and this rapid should be no problem for the average canoeist. As you and your boatmate glide through it, designate one person to cast to a small eddy on river left.

A long and fairly productive outside bend on river left now comes into view. This locale is a favorite one for those who spend the after-dark hours angling for flathead catfish. Some 20-pound-plus cats have come from this bend, and a goodly number of bass also dwell here. But the area receives too much fishing pressure to consistently produce three-pound and bigger mossy-backs. I am a strong advocate of catch-and-release for river smallmouths, and this area is a prime example of one that would benefit from that technique. People should especially release larger smallmouths—those over 15 inches. Such fish are not only the main spawners, but they are also the ones that have the best potential to reach trophy size.

The next major feature is a black railroad bridge that traverses the river. Two water willow beds lie just upstream from the bridge but only offer fair fishing. Shortly below the bridge is a tree-shaded bank on river right, but the water is too shallow to concentrate fish. Craigs Creek soon enters on river right, and a few strokes up Craigs sends you to the takeout. This access point requires that you haul your craft up a dirt path to a vehicle.

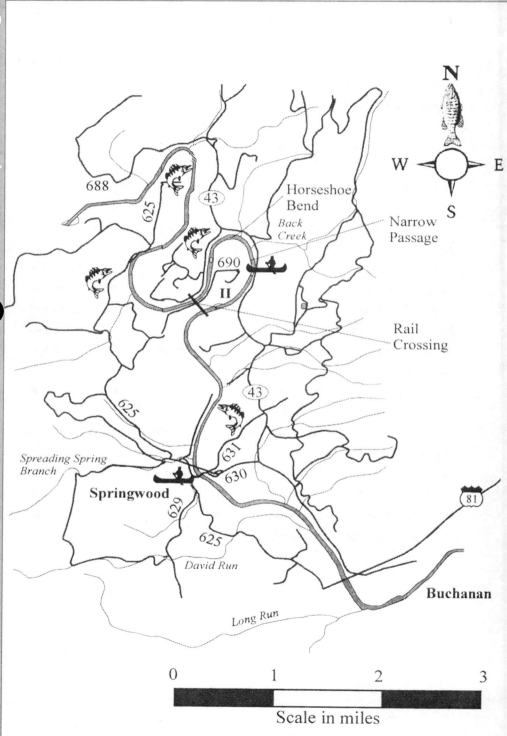

3 Eagle Rock to Narrow Passage

TRIP: Eagle Rock to Saltpetre Cave in Botetourt County

USGS QUADS: Eagle Rock, Salisbury, and Buchanan

DISTANCE: Thirteen miles

MAP: Opposite, page 62

RAPIDS: Several Class II rapids, numerous Class I rapids and riffles

ACCESS: At Eagle Rock, via Route 683 just off Route 220, lies the access point. Park your vehicle in the gravel parking lot, then haul your boat down a short, steep inline to reach Craigs Creek. Paddle down the creek a few yards to enter the James. A well-marked take-out is off Route 43 at Narrow Passage. The concrete ramp is on river left and is easy to spot. Parking spaces are plentiful in the gravel lot.

The Eagle Rock to Narrow Passage excursion is one of my favorites on the entire river. Because this trip is thirteen miles long, float fishermen should be prepared to spend a full day on the water. I have found that I usually must allot at least 11 hours to this trip; some days, because of the excellent action, I have pleasantly passed as many as 14 hours—and could have spent more. Canoeists will find this an outstanding day float. Be sure to budget time to take pictures of the Kanawha Canal ruins and the many beautiful vistas—this is one of the most scenic and isolated portions of the James. The last 11 miles of this float are part of the Virginia Scenic Rivers system.

Incredibly, outdoor enthusiasts of all persuasions almost lost this section of the James in the late 1980s when a developer proposed a dam. Not only would this have been a disaster for area wildlife, but also the dam would have been a great economic tragedy for Botetourt County and Southwest Virginia. People from all over Virginia and the Southeast come to the upper James, and the Eagle Rock float is the crown jewel of this section of the river. The loss of income to local merchants would have been significant. In the future, fishermen, canoeists, nature lovers, and bird watchers will undoubtedly have to work together to protect the James. They will also have to strongly make the case that the James is both an economic and natural resources asset as a free-flowing river.

At the beginning of the Eagle Rock trip, anglers have their choice of fishing a rocky shoreline on river right or a tree-lined bank on river left. Both areas receive considerable fishing pressure from bank and wade fishermen, and I often prefer to paddle on and begin fishing beyond the Eagle Rock Bridge (visible from the put-in) and the riffle area that immediately follows. Below the riffle area, some fair fishing commences. Journey to the left side of the river and cast to a bank replete with sycamores and silver maples. Next, look for an overhanging bluff on river right—a likely place to prospect for bass. The next bluff, however, signals the beginning of some extraordinary fishing. The shade of this rocky structure harbors some smallmouths, as do the rock outcroppings that line the bottom. The right side of the pool that borders the bluff supports excellent numbers of bass. I usually like to fish this area with topwaters on the initial pass, then paddle upstream beyond the bluff, and drift through the pool again in order to toss jig-and-pigs, plastic worms, and nymphs such as hellgrammite, stonefly, and dragonfly imitations.

Beyond this bluff appears another likely area as a small island, known as Peal's Island, cleaves the river. A Class I rapid and the remains of a Kanawha Canal lock distinguish the left side, and a rolling Class II rapid and an eddy characterize the right. If you take the left route, be sure to avoid the canal remains—the current tends to swing boats dangerously close to the lock. If you choose the right path, be prepared to take on some water because of the roller coaster effect of the rapid. Whichever side you choose, spend plenty of time in this area. Richard Furman, a good friend and my angling mentor, first showed me this pool and float trip as a whole when the aforementioned developer was planning to inundate this section. Furman cited this particular locale as one that would be ruined by the dam—a great loss to the river's fishery and its history because of the significance of the Kanawha Canal.

This pool continues downstream for well over 100 yards until it terminates in a riffle. But that riffle merely indicates the beginning of another smallmouth oasis: a long outside turn on river right. Plan on a good hour of fishing action in this bend. This is another big bass hangout on the Eagle Rock section, so try a variety of lure categories to determine which one is best for that particular day. The rock cover and undercut banks are simply outstanding fish habitat!

At this locale, I once met a group of float fishermen visiting from outside the region. The gentlemen told me that they were supposed to meet friends in

Buchanan in an hour or two and that they wanted to get in a lot of fishing before then. One individual asked me: "Just where are we anyway?" I explained that they were on the most isolated section of the headwaters of the James, that Buchanan was over 15 river miles away, and that they were going to be very late meeting their buddies. To prevent something like this from happening to you, always obtain a map of the James or any other river before planning a trip. I like to mark a map in one-mile intervals, so that I can wisely budget my time on the water. I know, for example, that on average I cover about one mile per hour while fishing and about 2.5 miles per hour while canoeing. Maps can show prime fishing areas such as outside bends and rapids as well as local landmarks, camping areas, and public land.

After this bend concludes, a long, deep straight stretch ensues. This expansive pool harbors good rock cover and a few sunken trees. Work a Carolina-rigged grub through the area; Clouser Minnows and deep-diving crankbaits perform well, too. Another island then appears; the right passageway offers the best route and has a Class I to II rapid. The left circuit is too narrow and shallow. Except during the spring when the water is up, fishing is poor around this rapid.

Catawba Creek, an important tributary, unites with the James in this area, and it also signifies that you are about six miles into this excursion. Actually, Catawba Creek enters in several places, dribbling in a little bit at a time on river right over several hundred yards. Beyond the previously mentioned island and rapid, a series of water willow beds and undercut banks on river left come into view. Several Class I rapids also pepper this section, making it another likely place to fish for bass.

Because of all the moving water through here, I often find bronzebacks active no matter what the season or the time of day. From late spring through early fall, I work Silver Outcasts and quarter-ounce Hart Stopper buzzbaits around the water willow beds and the current breaks. Rapidly-retrieved streamers, crankbaits and three-inch grubs account for fish, too. On one July float trip here, I witnessed just how effective buzzbaits can be for warm water river small-mouths. Although I caught a number of good bass that day on buzzers, one two-pound-plus smallie stands out. It charged from one of the water willow beds and followed the bait for some 10 yards, slashing at the buzzbait the entire time before finally engulfing it! Buzzbaits have that effect on bass.

Just when you think there could not possibly be any more exceptional bass habitat on the Eagle Rock float, a sensational outside bend looms on river left. This bend holds jumbo smallmouth and musky. I once witnessed a "Jaws" like attack of a three-foot long musky on a small carp here. My fishing companion, Mark Frondorff of Arlington, and I had spotted some surface commotion a short distance downstream. When we arrived near the site, a musky was ferociously assaulting a hapless carp. The phrase "blood on the water" rang true that day.

Some rock bluffs on river left mark the beginning of this bend and a rocky bottom extends directly from the shore. After fishing this area, paddle to the right and probe a long series of submerged logs, brush piles, and undercut banks. A few springs also trickle in, adding to the appeal. I sometimes make two passes through this bend because the habitat is so good. When this bend concludes, a number of rock ledges and grass beds appear on river right. Each of these sites offers

The author with a fine smallmouth that he caught on the Eagle Rock junket.

potential. Be sure to fish weighted nymphs and deep-running crankbaits out from this cover.

Next comes a series of easy Class I rapids, eddies, and deep water banks over the next several hundred yards. Passageways are numerous throughout.

The James courses along at a good pace through here, so make your casts count. The water moves too swiftly in many places for you to attempt a second cast at likely areas. This is also a great place to spot wildlife. Deer come down to the banks to feed and drink; wood ducks and mallards also make appearances.

Remarkably, there is yet another great fishing section to explore on this trip. A pair of rock bluffs and pools come into view on river right, and I have caught some nice bass from them over the years. These bluffs are wonderful places to work dry flies in the evening, which is often the time of day it is when you are at this juncture of the Eagle Rock float. The two crags and their accompanying pools also offer great photography potential.

This trip continues with a straight stretch of several hundred yards; railroad tracks and the community of Salt Petre Cave are on river left.

Next, you will come to a riffle that leads to a long rocky bank on river left. This bank continues for about 500 yards and affords some prime bronzeback cover. The composition here includes large boulders, basketball-sized rocks, occasional laydowns, and many cuts or indentations in the bank. In effect, you will work a series of mini-eddies through here, each one with the potential to produce a good fish.

Along the length of this bank a railroad track parallels the James. A point jutting out from river left terminates this section and sends the railroad track away from the James as well. I must point out that I almost drowned while fishing here one spring.

The time was early April and a good friend and I were making our inaugural float trip of the year. As is typical of the James in early spring, the river ran full that day and current quickly carried the canoe along. My friend, who was in the stern, decided to drag an anchor through the section to slow our pace and enable us to better work the left bank. Just seconds after my buddy dropped the anchor, it began to rake across the bottom—causing the boat to veer off course. I asked him to pull in the anchor, feeling it would wedge in the rocks. If an anchor becomes lodged on the bottom when a canoe is in swift water, then the anchor line becomes overly taut. This may cause the boat to whip dangerously back and forth, or even capsize. Almost as soon as my suggestion was made, the anchor lodged and seconds later we were dumped into the water. The air temperature was in the low 50s, as was the water temperature. Many veteran river fishermen say that if the air and water temperatures together do not total approximately 100 degrees, that nobody has any business being in the water. Although the air and water temperatures combined were above that magic number, my entire body felt as if it had received a punch from a heavyweight boxer when I landed in the stream.

My companion shouted for us to stay with the canoe, but I had already begun to feel numb, so I struck out for the shore, dragging along one fishing rod that I had managed to grasp when the craft capsized. In what seemed like an eternity, I reached the shore, exhausted. A few seconds later my friend, who had decided to abandon the boat after all, scrambled up on the bank beside me. We ran down the railroad tracks until we came to the point, where we retrieved his canoe as it drifted by. Amazingly, my camera case—a waterproof Pelican Mini dry box—was floating under the boat. Almost every other item of ours (including hundreds of dollars of fishing gear) was lost.

Spring is a great time to be on the James or any other river, but cold water can kill quickly, as we almost found out that day. Never drag an anchor behind a canoe in current. I now refuse to have an anchor in my Dagger Legend and try to discourage others from using them. I also always wear a life jacket the entire time I am on a river, regardless of the season. My friend and I were wearing life jackets that day. If we had not been, I doubt that we would have survived.

I have one addendum for the above episode. In 2008, 14 years after the anchor incident, I received a call from two anglers. They had been fishing the section where the anchor wedged in the rocks, had a lure snag on something, and one of them, having read this chapter, dove down to see what the lure was hung on. After much effort, the gentleman freed the anchor. The two men had called to ask if I wanted the anchor back.

I laughed out loud as if I would want the albatross back, but I certainly could not refuse the offer because of the herculean effort to retrieve the accursed thing. I went fishing with the two men a week later on the Maury River where they presented the anchor. It rested in my basement for a year, when, ironically, I received a magazine assignment on the brother of the man who owned the anchor. I gave the anchor to the brother who promised, in turn, to give it to his brother.

After the point, an easy Class I rapid appears, but channels are numerous. Check out the eddy on river right and the undercut bank on river left as the boat shoots through the rapid. The pool below is fairly shallow and offers only fair fishing. Next comes a series of riffles, eddies, and water willow beds on river right. All these areas hold a good bass or two, and this section is also a favorite for bank anglers—especially those after catfish at night. A short straight stretch next comes into view, then some Kanawha Canal remains on river left, followed by an approximately mile-long outside bend on river right. This is one of my favorite bends on the entire river and one where I first learned how effective soft plastic jerkbaits can be. It was the middle of a hot July day, and a friend and I had not experienced any success for several hours. I put on a Riverside Lures Big Gun, and smallmouth after smallmouth charged up from the depths to maul this fake minnow. I never go on a summertime trip down the James without a jerkbait.

This bend offers super rock cover along the bank and out from the shoreline as well. Several springs enter the river and they add to the appeal. In fact, even the inside bend of this area holds fish; a sycamore-choked bank provides shade during the middle of the day. Plan on spending well over an hour here.

A Class I rapid announces the end of this bend and then comes a likely bank on river right. Toss crawfish and nymph patterns and jig-and-pigs to the dropoffs that occur out from the points and water willow beds. A railroad bridge and a tunnel through a rock face on river right introduce the next section, known locally as Horseshoe Bend. Here you will find small islands, water willow beds, numerous riffles, and jumbo bass. Horseshoe Bend is a large feeding ground for fish. Fly-fishermen especially love this section, as excellent dry fly action can be found along the grass beds. Sneaky Pete poppers and grasshopper patterns can entice fish throughout the day. During the summer when water levels are low, some fly-fishermen even wade to here from the Narrow Passage ramp. Those who do so should hug the river left bank as the central channel is quite deep.

When the grass beds end, a series of dropoffs along the main channel begins. The water depth is well over ten feet and deep-diving crankbaits are just about the only lures that produce. Be sure to toss these artificials either upstream or across the current at a slight upstream angle. The goal is for cranks to deflect off the bottom and cause a reflex strike from a smallmouth. The last few hundred yards of the Eagle Rock float offer only mediocre fishing. Soon you will easily spot the Narrow Passage concrete ramp on river left.

Glen Wilton

Mill Creek

Gala

622

743

220

686

615

Craig Creek

43

Rail Bridge

Eagle Rock

818

43

688

692

682

687

II

Kanawha Canal Remains

809

220

Lapsley Run

726

731

688

Catawba Creek

681

655

612

622

N

W   E

S

625

43

Horseshoe Bend

Back Creek

Narrow Passage

690

II

Rail Crossing

625

43

0   1   2   3

Scale in miles

4 Narrow Passage to Springwood

TRIP: Narrow Passage to Springwood in Botetourt County

USGS QUAD: Buchanan

DISTANCE: Three miles

MAP: Opposite, page 70

RAPIDS: One difficult Class II, several riffle areas

ACCESS: At Narrow Passage, the concrete ramp put-in is off Route 43 on river left. Parking is plentiful in the gravel lot. The take-out is on river right under the Route 630 Bridge at Springwood. Parking is plentiful in the gravel lot. Take Route 876 off Route 630 to arrive at the bridge. **Note:** this access point is not suitable for motorized boats.

The delightful Narrow Passage float can take as long as six hours to fish or as short as three hours to paddle, depending upon how much time you spend seeking out the hot fishing spots. Canoeists should combine this trip with the downstream Springwood to Buchanan jaunt for a fun half-day on the river.

After the put-in, a long, deep-water riffle greets you on river left. Generally, I do not like to fish riffles because they typically hold only smaller bass under a foot long. This riffle is different because it sports both rocky cover and good water depth of four to six feet. Shallow water riffles, which I define as having depths of three feet or less, simply lack the overhead water column that gives gamefish the security to forage during daylight hours. Shallow water riffles also typically contain softball-sized and smaller rocks which can not provide sufficient cover for gamefish or large numbers of their prey such as sculpins, crayfish, and aquatic insects. Smallmouths will visit shallow water riffles during low light conditions, but they usually shun them on bright days.

The deep-water riffle at the beginning of the Narrow Passage float, however, concentrates large bass throughout the day. A good way to work this riffle is to designate one member of the canoe duo to man the craft and the other to cast upstream behind the boat. Numerous flies and lures work well for deep-water riffles. They include streamers and Murray's Hellgrammites, which can be retrieved with the current; crankbaits, which should be brought back quickly; jig-and-pigs, which can be hopped hurriedly along so as to avoid hang-ups; and grubs, which can be "popped" across the bottom in brisk bursts.

Given its inexpensive cost and the likelihood of hang-ups, a three-inch Kalin grub is probably the best choice. Rig a grub Texas style (weedless) with a quarter or three-eighths ounce sliding bullet sinker. When you feel this bait drag across the bottom, pop it immediately to avoid snags and to draw a reaction strike.

To the left of this riffle is a series of eddies, and over the years I have taken nice bass from each of them. Since you will be traveling quite fast by these pools, a topwater offering such as a Sneaky Pete popper or buzzbait is the best choice. Sometimes I will cast a Heddon Tiny Torpedo, Rebel Pop'R, or a grasshopper pattern to these backwaters, but I immediately retrieve them if I do not get a strike when they touch down. Letting a lure or fly linger in these pools will result in its loss. The current simply carries you along too quickly to allow a slow retrieve. After the series of eddies ends, look for some small pools and water willow beds on river left. They, too, hold fish, especially early and late in the day. This area is also a popular place for those after flathead catfish.

The next section is one of the most scenic on the upper James. Two large bluffs anchor the left shoreline and each borders a deep-water pool. Below

The Narrow Passage ramp at dawn on a summer morning.

the pools lies a Class II rapid, Ritchie's Falls, and several water willow beds. This is a superb area for outdoor photography, and I have taken numerous pictures here over the years. Adding to the appeal is the fact that the bluffs attract some jumbo mossybacks, but this area is not easy to fish. Smallmouths often cruise the wooded shoreline between the two bluffs during low light conditions, but they typically hunker in the depths for most of the day. A prudent strategy is to throw topwaters such as hair bugs, Jitterbugs, and Storm Chug Bugs on the first pass through the pool. Then paddle back and probe the deep water with weighted nymphs and plastic worms, craw worms, and lizards.

Ritchie's Falls rears up at the end of the second pool and is quite difficult to run on its left side, where the most water flows. Rocks jut up from the bottom throughout, making navigation a real challenge. I always run this rapid on far river right, where it is little more than a riffle. The right side is often quite shallow in the summer, so expect a bit of dragging to navigate through. Doing so is safer than trying to paddle through the rock maze on the left.

At most places on the James, whenever a pool/rapid/water willow bed sequence exists, great fishing occurs right below the grass. Sad to say, such is not the case below the vegetation here. The current has washed away all cover, and few gamefish, except for an occasional rock bass, dwell below the grass. You may wish to park your canoe at the bed and snap some photos of the gorgeous vistas upstream. I have sold several photos that were taken in this area, and the potential exists for any dedicated photographer to do the same.

An approximately 200-yard straight stretch now ensues, offering fair to good angling. But soon a railroad trestle crossing the river signals some good fishing in the current breaks that form behind the trestle supports. Below the trestle is an outside bend on river right; this area also has possibilities. A great deal of rocky cover lies along this bend, especially in the first part of it, and I have caught a number of quality fish here. The deep-water pool that stretches out from the bend also is worth checking, and I have had good success here with deep-running baits.

A riffle and some water willow beds mark the end of this bend and present some fair fishing. This juncture is another fine place to compose pictures. The area also introduces what is perhaps the best big smallmouth portion of the Narrow Passage float. On river left, for the next mile or so, lies some outstanding wood habitat. Laydowns, brush piles, old wood pilings, and a variety of other wood cover lie in great profusion throughout. In fact, I once encountered one of my biggest-ever James River smallmouths at a laydown here. A friend and I were tossing Tiny Torpedos toward a massive old sycamore tree that lay about a foot under water. A bronzeback roared up from under the tree, hit the Torpedo, and—incredibly—jumped over the log on the opposite side. The fish then steamed around under the log, and leaped over it again, wrapping the line around the cover twice. If a huge smallmouth wraps your line once around an object, you have virtually no chance to land the fish. But if a fish does so twice, you are surely doomed. A few seconds after the bass made its second go around the sycamore, my line snapped. My boatmate and I estimated that the fish went close to five pounds.

Besides Tiny Torpedos, other worthy baits to employ on this bank are Zara Spook Puppies, hair bugs, and fly rod poppers. I often will use both spin and fly-fishing gear to fish laydowns before I leave the area. Plan to work this particular shoreline at least 90 minutes or so. Don't waste time fishing the river right side, as it is too shallow to consistently concentrate fish.

The good fishing along this bank lasts almost to the take-out at Spring-wood. The Route 630 Bridge can be seen for a long way upstream from the access point, which is on river right directly under the structure.

⑤ Springwood to Buchanan

TRIP: Springwood to Buchanan in Botetourt County

USGS QUAD: Buchanan

DISTANCE: Four miles

MAP: Page 76

RAPIDS: No major rapids, several riffles

ACCESS: At Springwood, the put-in is on river right below the Route 630 Bridge. Route 876, which is off Route 630, leads to the put-in. The take-out is on river right just upstream from the Route 11 Bridge in Buchanan. After traveling south over the Route 11 Bridge, immediately turn right to arrive at the put-in. Parking is plentiful in the gravel lot; the ramp is concrete.

The Springwood to Buchanan trip is often the first one I take in the spring and the last one I enjoy in the fall. The reasons are simple. This section hosts no major rapids—a crucial factor when water temperatures are low and overturning a canoe could result in tragedy. Another plus is that the fishing on this float is consistently good from spring through fall. I have never caught a trophy smallmouth on the Springwood float, but I have landed a number of two-pound-plus fish. If you should encounter problems, Route 43 runs along the left bank during the first half of the trip, and Route 11 is close to the right shoreline on the second half, so help is always nearby.

Canoeists may want to couple this excursion with the Buchanan to Arcadia one, but float fishermen will find that they can easily spend five to six hours checking out the hot spots. Good fishing begins soon after the put-in. Within sight of the Springwood bridge is the first point of interest: a pair of water willow beds on river right. Some prime deep-water cover extends out from these beds as well. This area is a favorite of muskie fishermen, and over the years I have seen them land some fine specimens in the thirty-inch-plus range.

The next focal point is a long series of riffles and water willow beds that lie from the left shore to the center of the river. From spring through fall, this entire section is a marvelous place to work a streamer or a three-inch grub on a jig-head. Buzzbait and hair bug action can be outstanding during the summer. Channels are numerous and midstream boulders and rocks are easily spotted. Yet, and I confess this with great embarrassment, one of the worst accidents I have ever had on any river took place here.

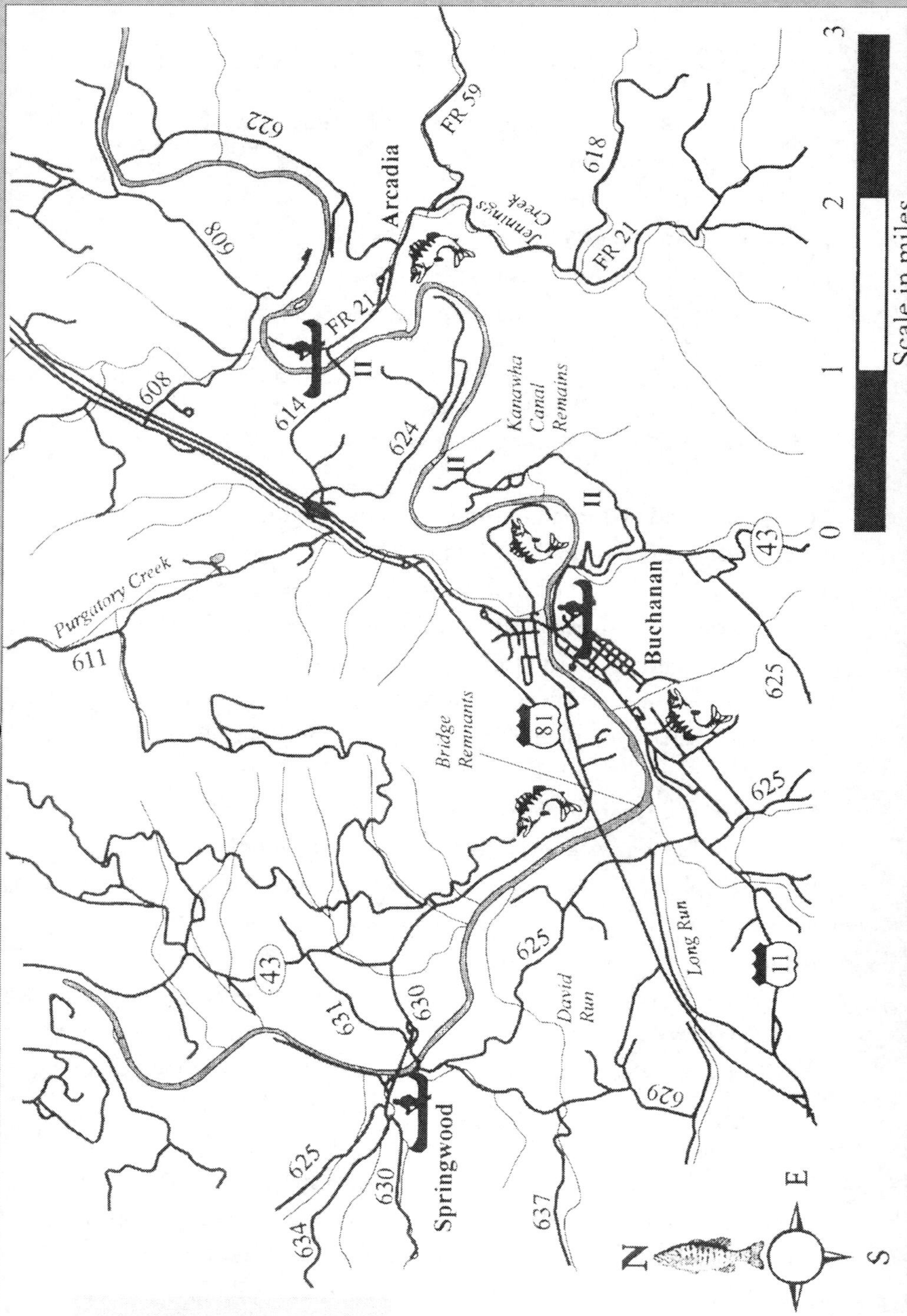

5
6

Scale in miles

0 1 2 3

Arcadia

622

FR 59

618

FR 21

Jennings Creek

608

FR 21

614

624

Kanawha Canal Remans

608

Purgatory Creek

611

Buchanan

43

625

Bridge Remnants

81

625

David Run

625

Long Run

43

631

630

625

630

629

637

634

Springwood

N
W   E
S

Paul Calhoun, a well-known photographer from Roanoke, my then ten-year-old-son Mark, and I were on an August canoe trip. We had easily made our way through the start of the riffles and were casting to likely spots. Since I was in the bow, I was the designated "watcher" for obstructions. But I was too intent on making casts to feeding bass, and suddenly we rammed a partially-submerged boulder—the only one in the area. My Dagger Legend canoe immediately broached, wrapping itself around the rock as all three occupants and their gear tumbled into the chilly water. My first concern was Mark, and I quickly grabbed him before he could be pinned between the canoe and rock. The canoe received a severe crease on one side, but we suffered no injuries and recovered all our gear. The important point, however, is that even though the Springwood float is the easiest one to negotiate of the trips on the headwaters, this trip, like any trip on any river, has obstacles. Those obstructions can cause an inattentive boater (as I was) to experience difficulty.

The next major feature is a rock bluff on river right. A deep water riffle/pool stretches out from the bluff, making this area an outstanding fishing hole. On one July raft trip, I tossed a quarter ounce buzzbait deep within the bluff's shadows and received the most jarring strike I have ever had from a smallmouth. When the bass slammed the blade bait, water sprayed everywhere. One of my boatmates exclaimed that surely a three-pounder had hit the lure while the other gentleman exclaimed that the fish might go four pounds. I, too, felt a whopper was on the line. The smallmouth charged toward the deep water riffle, wrapped the line around a boulder, and strained my spinning outfit to the maximum. Several minutes later I landed the fish—a 14-inch smallmouth that maybe went a pound and a quarter dripping wet. Although we were all surprised and thoroughly disappointed with the size of the fish, that smallmouth was a testimony to why these fish are the premier fresh water gamefish.

After the bluff, quickly paddle through some slow, flat water. The river then forms an outside bend on river left, and this is another superb area to chase after smallmouths. Most of this bend features either rock boulders in four to eight feet of water, undercut banks beneath sycamores and silver maples, or laydowns in deep water. The bend runs for a little less than a mile, but the left bank remains good to almost the Interstate 81 bridge that spans the James and indicates that you are about half way through the Springwood float.

Indeed, the left bank of this section is so bass-filled that I often make two passes through it. This is a great place to work crawfish patterns, jig-and-pigs, and four-inch plastic salamanders. If you are on this section early in the day, occasionally you will spot smallmouths feeding on the right side of the river as well. A number of laydowns dot the right bank, and sometimes I will paddle back and forth between the two sides. The right bank, though, is usually barren of fish after the sun rises high in the sky.

Just above the Interstate 81 Bridge, you will encounter some great deep water ledges and boulders. Try a weighted hellgrammite nymph or a Carolina-rigged grub or mini-crawfish here. Sometimes smallmouths can be drawn to the top by a fly rod popper or a soft plastic jerkbait. Below the bridge only mediocre fishing exists until you come to a pool above a riffle. The remains of a bridge support on river right mark this area as does Looney's Creek entering on river right. Those remains are a fine place to make a quick cast or two before the swiftly moving riffle sends you on your way. Actually the "bridge riffle" is just one of a series of riffles that characterize the next mile or so of the Springwood float. Besides those riffles, you will pass by water willow beds, shady banks, and eddies on river right, and some fair shoreline wood cover on river left.

I sometimes spend as long as two hours in this section; it is one that is productive throughout the morning, day, and evening from spring through fall. Deep-water riffles attract active bronzebacks. When one school of feeding fish leaves such an area, it is quickly replaced by another. I do best on this section with fast moving lures such as streamers, buzzbaits, crankbaits, and three-inch grubs on quarter ounce jig-heads. One friend of mine swears that Clouser Minnows were designed with this type of water in mind. Keep these flies and lures humming along and expect frequent strikes.

Once the riffle section terminates, some notable fishing still exists. The James slows and deepens and the muskie becomes the fish to catch. Muskie fisherman from all over the state come to the Buchanan ramp, launch their johnboats, and motor upstream to where the riffle ends in order to hurl eight-inch and longer minnow plugs. In fact, many anglers rate this section as some of the best muskie water in the entire Old Dominion. Flathead fanciers also relish the last few hundred yards of the Springwood float, and they are out in legion on summer nights. Bank anglers after cats also make their presence known on hot nights. All in all, this section has something for everyone except the whitewater lover. The take-out is easily spotted just upstream from the Route 11 Bridge in Buchanan. A concrete ramp welcomes you on river right.

The Springwood to Buchanan trip is popular with smallmouth and muskie anglers.

⑥ Buchanan to Arcadia

TRIP: Buchanan to Arcadia in Botetourt County

USGS QUAD: Buchanan

DISTANCE: Six miles

MAP: Page 76

RAPIDS: Several Class I and Class II rapids, several riffles

ACCESS: At Buchanan, the put-in is on river right just upstream from the Route 11 Bridge (see The Essentials section of preceding chapter). The take-out is on river right below the Route 614 Bridge near the community of Arcadia. The take-out is one of the most difficult on the James—you will have to haul your boat up a gravel incline of over 50 yards to a small gravel parking lot.

The Buchanan to Arcadia trip can last six to seven hours for float fishermen and can be a charming afternoon for canoeists. The only real negative about the Buchanan float is that it receives a tremendous amount of fishing and boating pressure, especially on weekends. This is because the Buchanan put-in is located less than five miles off Interstate 81 and is convenient for people traveling north and south through the Shenandoah Valley. If you plan to make this trip on the weekend, I recommend that you either put in at first light or the early afternoon to avoid the worst of the crowds.

After the put-in, paddle quickly under the Route 11 Bridge until you are several hundred yards below the structure. Some fair shoreline and bottom cover exists in this stretch, as does a riffle below the bridge, but they all receive such unending fishing pressure that anglers are better off beginning their casting downstream.

I like to start serious fishing right above the quarry located on river right. Soon after that, the river doglegs to the left and a Class II rapid appears. This rapid, known locally as the "Quarry Rapid," can be either very easy or quite difficult to negotiate, depending upon the amount of precipitation that has recently occurred. One cool April morning, Richard Furman, my river fishing guru, and I took the Buchanan excursion. The river ran high from spring rains and a steady wind blew from the northeast. When we rounded the bend above this rapid and saw it, we knew we were in trouble.

The Quarry Rapid flaunted several foot-high waves, running fast and rough. The wind had already begun to buffet Richard's canoe before we even

entered the top of the rapid. It was all we could do to keep the canoe headed
into the rapid. If the force of the river had ever turned the boat sideways in the
current, we would have capsized. Given the air and water temperature, hypothermia would have been a real possibility. When we finally made our way through
the Quarry Rapid, we had to paddle over to a river left sand-bar immediately
below to recover, physically and mentally. That day, the Quarry Rapid was
probably close to a Class III. By summer most years, this high-rolling rapid
has calmed to little more than a seesawing Class I. In any season, the best plan
is to hug the river left side and avoid the standing waves on the right.

Next you'll encounter a four-to-five-foot deep riffle section of some
one hundred yards. This section rarely holds large bronzebacks, but smallies in
the 12-to-14-inch range aggressively track down lures and flies. In the spring
and fall, try weighted crayfish patterns and crankbaits; in the summer and early
fall look to damsel and dragon flies and Tiny Torpedos. On hot summer afternoons here, the smallmouths seem to feast continuously on damsel and dragon
flies that flit too close to the surface. A rock-strewn bank lies on river right and

The Buchanan float begins in downtown but quickly becomes very rural in nature.

also demands some casts. Below this riffle area, an approximately one-mile-long outside bend on river left begins. Huge rocks, sycamore laydowns, and brush piles constitute the shoreline cover and are sanctuaries for sizable smallmouths.

What's more, this bend is productive throughout the fishing season. Wooly Buggers and jig-and-pigs are effective during the cold water period, and weighed nymphs and plastics perform well during the warm water months. Topwaters as diverse as buzzbaits and hair bugs account for fish during the summer and early fall. Here's a tip: the inside bend also has potential, which is a rarity on much of the river. The majority of inside bends on any river lack deep water and cover. However, toward the end of this inside bend on river right, a series of deep water laydowns speckle the shoreline. Cruise over to them, especially if they remain in the shade or low-light conditions exist, and cast fly rod poppers and Rebel Pop'Rs. Plan to spend a great deal of time in this overall area—it's the premier big bass hot spot on the Buchanan float.

The remains of the Kanawha Canal on river left and a Class II rapid signal the end of the bend. The water courses very swiftly through here and several boulders mottle the bottom. Run this rapid on river left to avoid the boulders and the heart of the rapid.

For the next mile or so, you will have to "hunt and peck" for small-mouths. At the start of this section, some boulders and undercut banks on river right offer refuge for smallies, and a few riffle areas harbor schools of minnows. For the most part, this portion holds few twelve-inch-plus fish and offers limited potential, especially on hot summer days when the sun unmercifully burns down on the water.

The river then forms a weak outside bend on river right and some fine fishing begins. Generally, the more pronounced a bend is, the better the fishing. This is because the water is deeper and there's a greater likelihood the current has deposited woody debris. Weak outside bends are typically better than inside bends in terms of fish-holding potential. This outside bend on the Buchanan float does offer numerous laydowns, but lacks great amounts of brush or rocky cover. Nevertheless, I have caught some above average fish here. One final note on this bend: its tail is its most outstanding section. You will spot a number of laydowns along the bank as well as some very deep water and an over-hanging sycamore canopy. Hair bugs, soft plastic baits, and jig-and-pigs are the best choices. Also of note is the fact that the Jefferson National Forest lies just beyond the railroad tracks that parallel this section on river right. Some outdoor enthusiasts like to camp on the right bank.

An island marks the beginning of the next section and presents canoeists with an interesting problem. The right route features a Class I rapid and some shallow water that may require portaging during the summer. The left side contains a Class I to II rapid that is tricky to run but offers better fishing. Generally, in the spring when the river is higher, I journey to the right side of the island. But in the summer, I prefer the left route. Be sure to work the eddy that rests at the end of this passage on river left.

The last half mile or so of the Buchanan float is very popular with wade fishermen, especially fly-fishermen. Jennings Creek enters in this section on river right. This section does not have much deep water—most of it lies in a column of three to four feet. This is a marvelous place to throw Sneaky Pete Poppers and hopper patterns for smallmouths in the one-pound range. Concentrate on the riffle area that comes at the very end of the trip. Larger fish are less common here.

The take-out on river right involves an overly long trek up a steep bank of over 50 yards. All in all, the charms of the Buchanan float are well worth the effort.

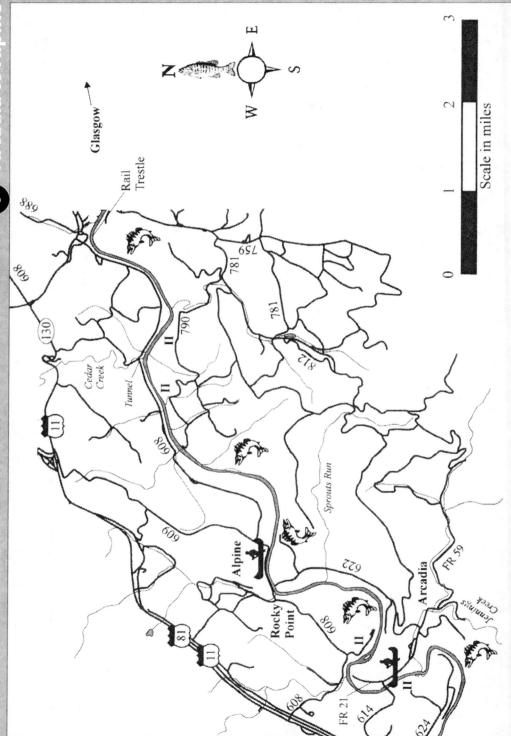

7 Arcadia to Alpine

TRIP: Arcadia to Alpine in Botetourt County

USGS QUADS: Buchanan and Arnold Valley

DISTANCE: Four miles

MAP: Opposite, page 84

RAPIDS: A Class II and several Class I rapids

ACCESS: The put-in is below the Route 614 Bridge near Arcadia. (*See* the gray box section of previous chapter.) The river left take-out is a small gravel parking lot on Route 608/622. This is a non-trailerable site. The actual put-in, which is across the road from the lot, is a gravel walkway leading to the river's edge.

Arcadia to Alpine makes for a sensational half-day float for the serious angler, especially the individual who likes the possibility of tangling with big bass. Canoeists should couple this trip with the preceding Buchanan to Arcadia float for a fun half-day excursion of about 10 miles.

This is also one of the most scenic sections of the James. Rocky Point, which is a majestic rock formation that juts out from the hillside above the river, occurs near the trip's end and is a favorite subject for many shutterbugs. You'll see remains of the Kanawha Canal, and everywhere, it seems, the wooded shoreline adds grace and beauty to this section. Bird watchers will find a wealth of species, from ospreys and red-tailed hawks to warblers and vireos. For those without a boat, wade fishing is possible both upstream and down from the Arcadia bridge. In fact, that area is a favorite for bank-bound fly-fishermen.

Richard Furman, a guide for Twin River Outfitters in Buchanan, loves the scenic nature of the Arcadia junket.

"One of my favorite parts of the float is the island below Arcadia," he said. "It's a true island in terms of size on the headwaters part of the river, and it also has a Kanawha Canal lock and abutment. There are even some pieces of hand-hewn timber in the river left over from the canal era."

For me, this section has special meaning because my initial visit to the river I love was here. A fellow teenager and I, both of us with our heads full of stories of the mighty James, came here many years ago. We seined hellgrammites from beneath the Arcadia bridge and spent an afternoon catching 10- to-13-inch smallmouths as well as rock bass and redbreast sunfish. That's when I became a forever fan of the James.

Some tremendous smallmouth sport is possible as soon as your paddle dips into the water. A long outside bend, extending about a mile and a quarter on river left, announces the beginning of the trip. And what a bend it is! Rock piles, boulders, log jams, submerged sycamores, and shoreline brush all dot the water's edge. Undercut banks and dropoffs are also a part of the shoreline, and at places the water is well over eight feet deep, which is considerable for the upper section of the James. The entire turn offers a wealth of fly and lure choices. One of my favorites is the summer topwater pattern.

On one August trip around this bend I scored by tossing an Arbogast Jitterbug toward the shoreline cover, aiming for the rocks and wood that lay beneath the sycamore, silver maple, and ironwood canopy. During the noon hour, a fine four-pound bronzeback ascended from the depths to lay waste to the Jitterbug. This lure has an amazing ability to draw up large fish even during the heat of the dog days. Retrieve the bait just fast enough so that it leaves a small wake behind it. Smallmouths often track Jitterbugs for long distances—something they will rarely do for other topwaters. Therefore, this is one artificial that should be retrieved all the way to the gunnel.

The scenic Alpine float is a great getaway.

Other fine topwater offerings for this bend and others include Heddon Tiny Torpedos, Rebel Pop'Rs, Phillips Crippled Killers, Hart Stopper buzzbaits, and Storm Chug Bugs. The overgrown shoreline looks just like the sort of place where terrestrial creatures will blunder into the water. To take advantage of this, fly-fishermen should consider hair bugs such as those which imitate mice, frogs, and hoppers. Many river anglers only toss topwaters early and late in the day. But prime areas such as bends often offer topwater action during the heat of the day.

Over halfway through this bend a sand bar and a short riffle cleave it. The sand bar and riffle often attract active, aggressive smallmouths, so be sure to work the area thoroughly. An easy Class I rapid and a long, narrow eddy on river left herald the end of the bend and offer good fishing as well. I like to run this rapid on the far right so as not to spook the fish in the eddy, then allow its reversing currents to capture my canoe. I stay within the eddy until I have probed its underwater cover thoroughly. However, if you are just paddling the Arcadia float, run this rapid on the far left. For point of reference, the general area is known as Indian Rock.

Next come some remains of the Kanawha Canal on river left, and the structure here is one of the more visible and photogenic of the canal remnants. An island and its accompanying Class II rapid lie below the remains and demand attention. The right passageway is typically too shallow and rocky, offering the real possibility of damage to a canoe, so take the left route and be prepared to maneuver around some midstream rocks. The fairly deep pool resting below the Class II is an especially inviting pool for fly-fishermen because various may fly hatches can be viewed here throughout the late spring and summer.

The next two miles feature three Class I rapids and all offer superb fishing below them. These are basically "cookie cutter" rapids—all offer plenty of passageways, none require tricky maneuvers, and smallmouth bass inhabit the current breaks within. Overall, I would rate the first Class I as having the best habitat; be sure to investigate the deep bank that borders it on river right. The latter two rapids probably provide better mid-stream cover in the form of submerged rocks. For smallmouths in current, I recommend streamers, buzzbaits, grubs, and shallow-running crankbaits such as the Cordell Big O and Storm Wiggle Wart. Three-inch Kalin grubs, threaded onto a quarter-ounce jig, work well because of their lifelike tails and soft texture.

The last half of the Arcadia float meanders along at a pleasant pace, and the river and its wooded shoreline continue to be quite scenic, but the fishing is not as good as it is on the first leg of this journey. The shoreline habitat is quite unremarkable until you come to the Rocky Point area, which is within a few hundred yards of the take-out. A river left bend begins several hundred yards up from Rocky Point. I have caught a number of good small-mouths from this bend, but the initial bend of the Arcadia float is still, by far, the best one on this trip. At the end of the turn, you will spot Rocky Point and a feeding flat composed of large rocks and some wood in three to four feet of liquid. Be sure to toss topwaters to this flat.

After you leave the feeding ground, you will enter a short riffle and then will spot railroad tracks on river left. All that remains of this section is a few hundred yards of rather mediocre fishing, and I usually make only a few token casts. As a whole, though, the Arcadia float is one of the James' premier destinations for river lovers of all kinds.

⑧ Alpine to Glasgow

TRIP: Alpine to Glasgow in Botetourt and Rockbridge counties

USGS QUADS: Arnold Valley, Snowden, and Glasgow

DISTANCE: Ten and one-half miles

MAP: Page 90

RAPIDS: Several Class I and Class II rapids

ACCESS: At Alpine, the river left put-in is near a small gravel parking lot on Route 608/622. This is a non-trailerable site. The actual put-in, which is across the road from the lot, is a gravel walkway leading to the river's edge. The Glasgow river left take-out is at Locher Landing. The Maury enters on river left at this spot as well. Parking is available in a gravel lot. The access point itself is a canoe slide with a 50-yard or so gravel path leading to it from the parking lot. This is a non-trailerable site.

The Alpine float is yet another remarkable destination on the upper river that offers a great deal for the angler, canoeist, and photographer. Although this section receives a tremendous amount of boating traffic on weekends, owing to the fact that several canoe liveries are nearby in Natural Bridge and Buchanan, it is still a fine getaway, particularly on weekdays.

I suggest that fishermen allot a full 10-hour day here. Although this section lacks the pronounced outside bends so common for the upper river, it does have a number of deep-water sanctuaries, an abundance of water willow, and plenty of Class I to II drops. The Alpine float is also ideal for a paddler of intermediate skills—just enough rapids to add spice to a trip, but not so many that one does not have time to enjoy the wooded banks, wildlife, and the James itself. For camera enthusiasts, some of the most scenic remains of the Kanawha Canal to be found on the part of the James covered by this book lie on this float. In addition, the Jefferson National Forest parallels the right bank for much of the section, and you'll find a number of places to camp or enjoy shore lunches. Because of these sights and varied activities, canoeists on multiple-day trips may want to make this float part of their itinerary. Paddlers out for the day may want to spend all of it on this section.

The trip begins with an easy Class I rapid immediately below the put-in. Surf through the small, standing waves and enter a short, narrow pool. Soon afterwards, an easy Class I ledge with easily-spotted passages follows. Great deep-water habitat characterizes this section; in fact, the entire first mile of this

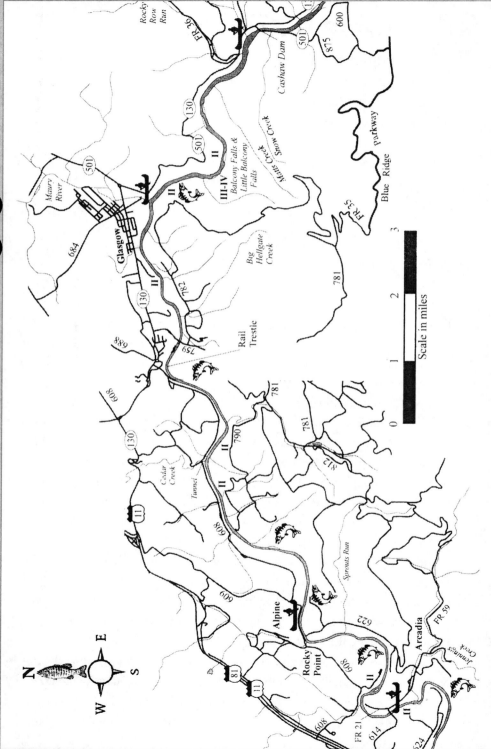

Scale in miles

0   1   2   3

N
W   E
S

float provides mid-river sanctuaries for smallmouths. If you are on this section early or late in the day, a good strategy is to fish the laydowns on river right and the water willow beds on the left. Any other time, however, I recommend retrieving weighted crayfish and hellgrammite patterns, and Texas-rigged plastic worms, craw worms, and lizards through the heart of the deep water. Boat traffic here tends to keep the fish deep for much of the day during the warm-water period.

The next major feature is the remnants of the Kanawha Canal on river left. The remains tower above the river and also create a ledge across the stream. For picture opportunities, I like to paddle to an island on river right, beach the canoe, wade out toward the structure, and explore different camera angles. The canal creates a Class I to II drop, and the best passageway is on far river left within the shadows of the structure. During low water conditions, you may also drag your canoe through some shallows adjacent to the left side of the island. I have enjoyed some solid action just below this rapid. Look for small-mouths to be chasing minnows throughout a summer day. A fairly deep pool lies beyond the rapid, but it offers only mediocre fishing.

For the next three miles or so, until you reach the Gilmore Mills area, you will encounter only one Class II rapid. This rapid flaunts a precipitous drop of about three feet and is best run through a chute on far river left. On one August trip my partner and I almost became stuck in the chute. Check water levels before selecting a passage. Immediately below this rapid, you'll find some great wade fishing. Be sure to work Clouser Minnows, crankbaits and grubs through the pool on river right; buzzbaits and Sneaky Pete Poppers also produce here. Some gorgeous mountain scenery exists in this area. I like to wade downstream from the rapid and take pictures of the ridges and rapid. A particularly interesting composition is to shoot upstream when someone runs the rapid. The splendid upland habitat behind the rushing water creates a back-drop of almost postcard quality. Although the rapid is the predominant feature on this part of the Alpine float, wonderful fishing can be found throughout. Look for laydowns on both sides of the river and numerous water willow beds. Summertime fly-fishermen especially relish this section because of the damselfly and dragonfly activity.

Five miles into the Alpine excursion, you reach the community of Gilmore Mills on river left. A tunnel on that side marks the section and is also where Cedar Creek enters the James. Some superior deep-water smallmouth cover is found in this area, and anglers should slowly drag weighted nymphs and plastic baits through here. The hamlet of Gilmore Mills, through which you will pass through while running the shuttle, is a reminder of decades past. Consider taking pictures of an abandoned two-story mercantile-like building in "downtown" Gilmore Mills, which surely must have been the focal center of the community in a bygone era.

A mile or so below Gilmore Mills is a Class II. I prefer to run it on the far left, but other paddlers I know opt for the middle or far right. Water levels and river conditions can create some confusion about how to slide through this rapid, so follow safety precautions and scout the rapids before attempting to dash through them. This step, of course, should be taken on all major rapids on any river.

For much of the next two miles, you will encounter some simply marvelous deep-water cover. Depths of over ten feet exist in this section. It was on this portion of the Alpine float that I first learned the benefits of the Carolina rig for deep-water river bass. The Carolina rig, which consists of a half-ounce egg

This muskie came from the Alpine trip, one of many on the James where this member of the pike family flourishes.

sinker, bead, swivel, two-foot-long leader, and a grub, lizard, or craw worm, has traditionally been a favorite of lake bass fishermen. River anglers have typically ignored this system. Nevertheless, no other rig will get your bait to the bottom and keep it there—where the big smallmouth hunker—like the Carolina rig. Use it on this section—and hang on!

The next mile or so of the float is a favorite of muskie anglers. A black railroad bridge, which looks as if it is bowed in the middle (an optical illusion) serves as a landmark.

For much of the rest of the trip, the James River Face Wilderness Area is on river right. This wilderness area is one of the most pleasurable hiking places in the Old Dominion. My favorite part of the Face is the Devil's Marbleyard—a jumble of mammoth boulders on the side of a mountain. A number of inviting trails beckon the backpacker—try the one that leads to the Balcony Falls Trail Head.

An outside bend exists next, but it does not contain the amount of wood and rock cover that many bends on the James do. However, out from the bend is some solid deep water habitat. For years, I pounded the banks of this float, casting to bits of cover here and there. But better cover and fishing can be found away from the banks on this section as a whole. The trip's major rapid is a challenging Class II that requires some maneuvering. An old tower on river left helps mark the area. This rapid is best scouted from a rock ledge above it, where paddlers can carefully examine the route. The preferred path is usually right down the center. Although this is certainly a stimulating rapid to run, more and better whitewater looms downstream on the Glasgow to Snowden trek.

The take-out on river left is easily spotted, hard above where the Maury River enters the James.

TRIP: Glasgow to Snowden in Rockbridge, Bedford, and Amherst counties

USGS QUADS: Glasgow and Snowden

DISTANCE: Five and one-half miles

MAP: Page 90

RAPIDS: The famed Class III-IV Balcony Falls, numerous Class I and Class II rapids

ACCESS: See the gray box of the previous chapter for the put-in. The river left take-out is along Route 130 above Cushaw Dam. You will have to paddle under a small bridge and up Rocky Row Run to reach the concrete ramp and gravel parking lot.

For the white water thrill seeker, the Glasgow float is the best excursion on the headwaters section of the James On this river, the best white water exists where a pronounced change in geology occurs, and that happens part way through this excursion. Here the James transitions from a mountain stream to a Piedmont stream, with the precise location being the Class III-IV Balcony Falls. (Farther downstream, a series of rapids above the fall line at Richmond is the only rival to this white water on the James.)

The allure of Balcony Falls is felt across the Old Dominion, and thousands of fast water devotees make a pilgrimage to this section every year. Here you'll also find numerous other rapids and some unsurpassed smallmouth bass fishing as well. Float fishermen and canoeists/kayakers should allot a half day to this float. Fishermen will want to linger in the many eddies below rapids, and paddlers will desire to run Balcony several times or tarry in its hydraulics. Outdoor photographers will revel in the mountain scenery on river right and in several different sets of Kanawha Canal remains on river left.

Twin River Outfitters' guide Richard Furman relishes this excursion. "The reason I like this trip so much is not just because of the fishing, but also there is no question in my mind that I have yet to see a sight on the James River more beautiful than Balcony Falls early in the morning or late in the evening," he said. "You are in this huge, huge gorge and realize how small you are when this majestic rapid rears up—well, that is something to cherish."

The rapids and great fishing begin immediately. Within sight of the put-in, you will immediately encounter a Class I rapid, Fork Falls; run it on the left and be sure to fish the backwater on the same side. This is an excellent place to work streamers, grubs, and tube baits.

Next comes a marvelous opportunity for photographing Kanawha Canal remains. Smallmouth bass love to hang out in the shadows of this structure; cast Wooly Buggers and plastic worms to its base. Soon afterwards, you will find a number of mid-river boulders and then a Class I-II rapid, Flat Rock Falls. The best passageway is right down the middle. Cast to the downstream side of those boulders before running the rapid. Also, if you undertake the Glasgow float during warm weather, these boulders make ideal perches from which to take pictures. A wide-angle lens is best.

More rapids await. Several Class I ledges appear, followed by yet another Class II ledge. None of these rapids are too demanding for the intermediate paddler, and they are a great deal of fun to run. The fishing is great through here as well; cast buzzbaits and dry flies (especially damsel and dragon fly patterns) to the pools directly above these rapids. The sweet casting spot is the "lip" immediately above where the river begins its descent into swift water.

Jeff Kelble and guide Britt Stoudenmire celebrate a nice smallie caught on a fly rod near Balcony Falls.

Below the Class II ledge, Little Balcony Falls by name, is yet another stone canal wall, and here I enjoyed some of the most spectacular smallmouth action I have ever experienced. On a summer trip with Dick Pickle, who operates the Wilderness Canoe Company in Natural Bridge, I caught four two-pound smallmouths in five casts from that wall. All the bass hit a quarter-ounce Hart Stopper buzzbait, and all jumped repeatedly. In fact, that day I battled a dozen smallmouths between two and four pounds in just five hours of fishing. Pickle says that such action is common on this float, mainly because the rapids make it inaccessible to many fishermen. But if you are an expert paddler or if you hire an outfitter, the Glasgow trip is a must!

Balcony Falls is the next attraction, some one and one-half miles into the trip. A long rocky ledge extends from the river right bank and makes for a good place to scout the rapid. The mountain scenery on the right bank is also a marvelous reason to linger awhile. I must admit that I always undergo a little bit of trepidation before I run Balcony. The overall feeling that I experience when beginning this rapid is that of being launched out into space. Regarding portaging Balcony, options are very limited and really no satisfactory one exists. This is what I do. As I approach Balcony Falls in a canoe or kayak, I maneuver over to river right and debark from the boat. I then drag the canoe or kayak over and around, up and down, some boulders. With a canoe, I have to have help and assistance is much appreciated with a kayak. Please strongly consider portaging this rapid; paddlers have perished here. That said, the best route is a chute to the left of a partly submerged rock in the middle. This rock can overturn a boat, so be sure to locate it before entering the rapid. Some large surfing waves follow, and they too can topple a craft. Kayakers, however, are drawn to these waves and I have seen them spend ten minutes or more "surfing" in them.

Tobacco Hills Falls and Velvet Rock Falls must be dealt with next. This Class II rock garden can be run from a variety of directions. I prefer the river left route. Angling is excellent through here. On one visit, I caught a four-pound bronzeback from behind a boulder below Tobacco Hills Falls. The good fishing continues for several hundred yards below Little Balcony as numerous large rocks stud the river. Fishermen may want to spend an hour or more casting to these obstructions. Unfortunately, the great fishing and white water then come to an end because of the effects of Cushaw Dam—the first of seven dams between Snowden and Lynchburg. The last two miles or so will be spent paddling—typically into a stiff wind—to the take-out. Some good largemouth bass action is possible in this area, especially in the winter and spring.

The New River Gorge in West Virginia is the home of some of the best white water in the United States and those rapids draw thousands of tourists and pump millions of dollars annually into that state's economy. I have often speculated that if the first of those seven dams had not been constructed, Virginia likewise might have enjoyed similar economic benefit because of outdoor recreation. Sadly, developers and politicians rarely understand the monetary benefits of outdoor recreation and often blindly approve dams in the name of "progress." The Glasgow trip ends at the Snowden take-out.

The James Between the Dams

10 Bedford Dam to Bedford Dam 98

11 Bedford Dam to Hunting Creek 102

12 Big Island to Big Island 107

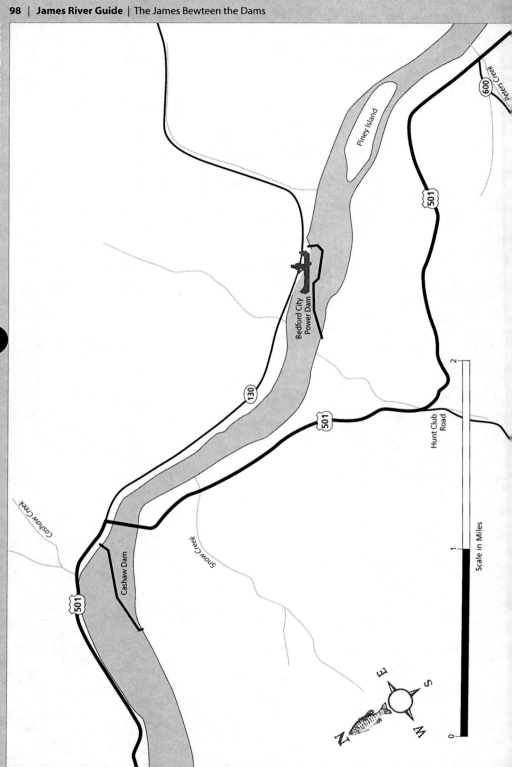

10 Bedford Dam to Bedford Dam

TRIP: Bedford City Power Dam to Cushaw Dam to Bedford City Power Dam in Bedford and Amherst counties

USGS QUADS: Big Island and Snowden

DISTANCE: One mile up and one mile back

MAP: Opposite, page 94

RAPIDS: Riffles

ACCESS: At Bedford City Power Dam, a river left access point exists above the dam warning buoys. You will have to haul your canoe or kayak across Route 130, then over a guardrail to reach the access point, which is to the left of a concrete dock. Parking consists of a gravel pull-off on Route 130. This is a non-trailerable site.

The Bedford City Power Dam junket is a very interesting float in that you access the river at the same place you take out. My preferred way to float this section is to slowly paddle up the river left side to the tailrace of Cushaw Dam, a distance of about one mile, next debark from my canoe and wade fish a while then float back by fishing on river right. Last, I paddle back across the James to the river left access point. That way, I am able to work both shorelines and can even cast to quite a few mid-river holding areas.

Interestingly, Jared Harker, who operates Confluence Outfitters, told me that he prefers the opposite approach and likes to paddle on river right up to the dam, then scoot down the left shoreline. After Jared and I debated our various reasons for our respective routes, I came to the conclusion that our decision for floating this section the way we do was based more on tradition than logic.

Jared states that although this section is not known for its citation smallies and muskies, plenty of good size fish exist. Harker and his clients have caught a number of smallies in the 12- to 16-inch range and muskies approaching 40 inches have been landed as well.

No rapids exist throughout, but throughout the voyage upstream, you will encounter a series of riffles. When navigating upstream, I like to to paddle and fish for 50 to 100 yards at a time, then lodge the canoe against one of many boulders, water willow beds, or above water ledges that characterize the river left side. Once docked, I either remain in the canoe, stand on a rock, or wade fish and thus thoroughly work an area. This is a very slow, painstaking method to fish, but it is the best way, I believe, to work this James River float. For example, on one junket with Paul Hinlicky, a Roanoke College religion professor, he caught smallmouths up to 15 inches while I caught a trio of fish in the 12-to-14-inch range. Not an epic day by any means, but, nevertheless, a very satisfying one.

Hinlicky experienced his most consistent success with a ¼-ounce buzzbait, as the water temperature registered in the upper 70s. Interestingly, as is so often the case on the James and other Western Virginia rivers, the buzzbait bite did not become full fledged until after noon. Indeed, I purposefully did not ply a buzzer until I noticed that brown bass started to track Paul's bait. For whatever the reason on the James, the buzzbait bite seems to materialize slowly but consistently with the bass going through successive stages of being more and more aggressive until they at last begin to latch onto the lure. After Paul finally caught one on his buzzer, I too was able to catch a quality fish. The buzzbait mode of the fish lasted about 90 minutes and then it was over. All in all, Hinlicky, who lives in Roanoke County, and I took about four hours to paddle and fish up to Cushaw Dam.

Cushaw Dam is the first one on the upper river.

After you reach the tailrace of Cushaw Dam, you have two options. The end of the tailrace, which lies in the vicinity of the Route 501 Bridge, also flaunts a Class III rapid on river right (the dam lies on river left). You can debark from a canoe and wade this area or even wade up along the river right bank and fish above the Class III. Or you can immediately turn your craft around and begin the float back to the Bedford Dam access point.

Paul and I chose the former option before heading back downstream. On the way back to the Bedford Dam access point, there are really only two landmarks of note on river right: where Snow Creek enters and where the old Snow Creek Culvert sits. Both of these occur at the very beginning near the Route 501 Bridge. The river right stretch features the occasional downed tree and rock pile.

However, the best cover and structure exists in the mid river reaches where numerous boulders, ledges, and dropoffs characterize the bottom. My advice is to move well off the shore and for the next mile work crankbaits and Carolina rigs through this rock cover. The Bedford Dam float is an interesting one that requires considerable amount of work and paddling to undertake, but it is a rewarding excursion, nevertheless.

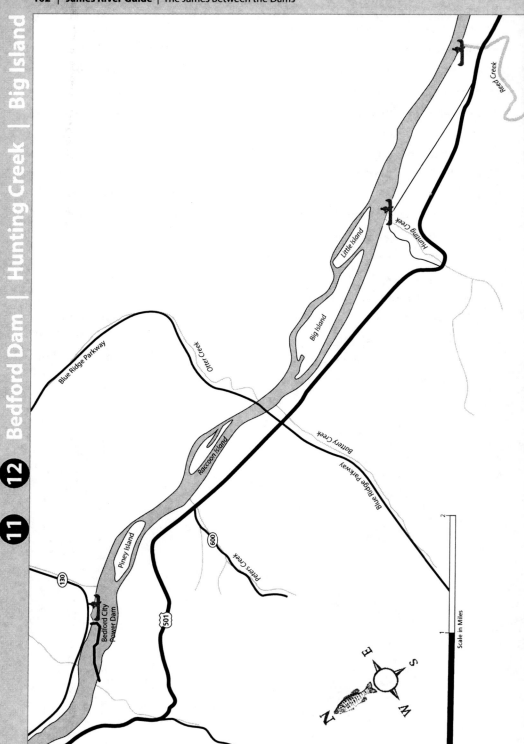

11 Bedford Dam to Hunting Creek

TRIP: Bedford City Power Dam to Hunting Creek in Bedford and Amherst counties

USGS QUADS: Big Island and Snowden

DISTANCE: Three miles

MAP: Page 102

RAPIDS: Class IIs, Is, riffles

ACCESS: At Bedford City Power Dam, a river left access point exists above the dam warning buoys. You will have to haul your canoe or kayak across Route 130, then over a guardrail to reach the access point, which is to the left of a concrete dock. Parking consists of a gravel pull-off on Route 130. This is a non-trailerable site. After entering the water and paddling across the James, you will have to haul your canoe up a steep bank covered with scouring rushes, then along railroad tracks, and down a steep, rocky bank to a channel that exists below the dam. This is a very strenuous portage. Above Big Island Dam, a river right concrete ramp exists called the Boat Ramp at Hunting Creek Towpath Bridge. You will have to paddle under the bridge to reach the ramp, which exists at the end of Riverside Circle via Route 501. Parking spaces are numerous in a gravel lot.

The Bedford City Power Dam float is roughly divided between smallmouth and largemouth water with the brown bass dominating the upper portion and the bigmouths the lower. Smallmouth anglers should undertake the portage (and it is a difficult one around Bedford Dam) while largemouth fans should debark in their motorized boats from the Hunting Creek access point and travel upstream.

The tailrace below Bedford Dam consists of very strong currents, and paddlers should be careful to avoid them. When the tailrace slows, though, the well-aerated water draws smallmouths, rock bass, and redbreast sunfish. And when the water slows even more, you should be prepared to duel with muskies. In fact, Jared Harker who operates Confluence Outfitters, says that this trip conceals some of the biggest muskies on the James with 40-inch monsters lurking in the depths. Jared says this float also can offer up smallmouths that top three pounds. It's easy to understand why when the bass habitat is considered.

A number of braided channels (an uncommon though welcome habitat form in much of the upper river) exist below the dam, and Class II and I rapids appear throughout for several hundred yards. One of the Class IIs is of such significant force that you may want to portage. Huge boulders also litter the bottom, and water willow islets are common. Below the braided channels lies Piney Island and a series of riffles. The best passageway is on the left side. This, too, is an excellent place to fish for smallmouths. Rock bass and sunfish can be found finning the backwaters.

Below Piney Island lies more boulders, especially on the river left side, and numerous riffles as well. Next looms Raccoon Island. Both passages feature riffles and boulders and great action for smallmouths. A Blue Ridge Parkway bridge then crosses the river, and this structure roughly divides the smallmouth

Excellent and underpublicized fishing exists below Bedford Dam.

and largemouth sections of the float—although, of course, both species can be caught above and below. Motorized boaters will have no trouble traveling up river to this point.

Big Island soon appears and extends for well over a half mile. The better passageway is on the left side where boulders and gentle riffles greet you. Toward the end of Big Island comes Little Island, you will need to scoot down the right side of the smaller land mass. Laydowns and backwaters characterize this section, and largemouth bass and bluegills predominate. After you leave Little Island, maneuver over the river right side, and look for a bridge that extends over Hunting Creek. Run up Hunting Creek to the take-out point.

⓬ Reed Creek to Big Island Dam and Back

TRIP: Reed Creek to Big Island Dam

USGS QUAD: Big Island

DISTANCE: Three/fourths of a mile up, then return

MAP: Page 98

RAPIDS: Riffles

ACCESS: On river right, a concrete ramp exists where Reed Creek enters. A gravel parking lot is off Route 501.

This is the shortest float on the entire James, as it consists of putting in at a ramp, paddling up to a Class I, then returning the three-fourths of a mile to the access point. Guide Richard Furman says that it is very difficult to paddle above the Class I rapid that lies below the dam as the water is quite swift. Obviously, this is not an all-day adventure, but if you are looking for an afternoon excursion that offers the opportunity to joust with smallmouths, largemouths, and muskies, this is a trek worth considering.

I've caught some very nice smallmouth on the Big Island float and Jared Harker of Confluence Outfitters says that some jumbo muskies hunker down in the deep pools. You can also paddle downstream for several hundred yards and ply the shorelines for largemouths. Because this is such a short trip and chapter, I wanted to include information about a group devoted to protecting the river's watershed, the James River Association (JRA).

According to chief executive officer Bill Street, the JRA has served as the leading voice for protecting the river and takes action to promote conservation and responsible stewardship of its natural resources. The James River Association (JRA) was founded in 1976 as a member-supported river conservation organization by a group of citizens who were concerned about the health of the James River and wanted to have an active role in its future. Today, JRA continues to be the only organization in Virginia working solely to protect and enhance the James River and the 15,000 miles of tributaries that flow throughout its 10,000 square mile watershed.

To address river health issues throughout the watershed, JRA engages partners including corporations, local governments, farmers, landowners, individuals and state and national agencies. Through these partnerships JRA identifies root causes of pollution in the watershed and implements solutions to reduce or eliminate their negative impacts. In doing so, JRA provides educational and volunteer opportunities to engage citizens of all ages to restore and protect America's Founding River.

Through a broad base of innovative programs JRA engages the public to become aware of and actively involved in conserving the James River and its tributaries for future generations to enjoy. Here are some of the core programs:

James RIVERKEEPER—The James River Riverkeepers are the eyes and ears of JRA on the river, assessing its condition and responding to problems as they arise. The Upper James Riverkeeper and Lower James Riverkeeper are on-the-water advocates monitoring the river for pollution and working with volunteers, including boaters, fishermen, farmers and landowners, to investigate reports of pollution, promote awareness of water-related issues and foster good stewardship for a cleaner, healthier river.

The Big Island float is short but it can be fruitful as Tim Wimer discovers.

Outreach—JRA's Outreach Program connects individuals and communities with their local portion of the James River and connects communities watershed-wide through river-corridor planning and conservation initiatives. JRA is working with partners such as National Geographic and local groups to provide more river access points to increase opportunities for individuals to enjoy and appreciate the river.

Environmental Education– JRA's education programs help students connect with the river to instill a sense of interconnection with the natural world and the James River ecosystem. In 2013, JRA opened the James River Ecology School on Presquile National Wildlife Refuge, a partnership with the U.S. Fish and Wildlife Service, where they provide experiential learning programs designed introduce students and educators to the James River and how to be river stewards.

Watershed Restoration—JRA engages volunteers to implement solutions throughout the watershed to improve river health. The public has opportunities to participate in hands-on projects designed to educate citizens and prevent runoff by implementing projects such as stream buffer restoration, rain gardens, rain barrels and trash cleanups.

River Advocacy—JRA works with policy makers on the local, state and federal levels throughout the watershed to ensure that the river is fully considered in policy matters that affect its health and to advocate for policy solutions to address critical issues facing the river.

For more information about the James River and the James River Association, go to www.TheJamesRiver.org.

Upper James

13 Scotts Mill Dam to Six-Mile Bridge 110

14 Six-Mile Bridge (Lynchburg) to Joshua Falls . . 114

15 Joshua Falls to Riverville 117

16 Riverville to Bent Creek 125

17 Bent Creek to Wingina 129

18 Wingina to James River WMA 135

19 James River WMA to Howardsville 138

20 Howardsville to Scottsville 143

Scale in miles

3 2 1 0

Beck Creek

622

Joshua Falls Dam

Remains of dam

Remains of dam

Joshua Falls Dam

664

Joshua Falls

Nine Mile Bridge (Rail)

726

609

659

Six Mile Bridge (Rail)

Buzzard Islands

Feagan's Island

Setting Pole Falls

672

460

Little Opossum Creek

Opossum Creek

29

766

683

684

685

Reusens Dam

Judith Creek

Harris Creek

Woodruff Island

Treasure Island

Ivy Creek

Daniel Island

Scott's Mill Dam

Winston's Island Stay Left

Tomahawk Creek

Blackwater Creek

Lynchburg

N E W S

13 Scotts Mill Dam to Six-Mile Bridge

TRIP: Scotts Mill Dam to Six-Mile Bridge in Amherst and Campbell counties

USGS QUAD: Kelly

DISTANCE: Six miles

MAP: Opposite, page 110

RAPIDS: One Class I and riffles

ACCESS: Below Scotts Mill Dam, the river left concrete ramp is just off River Road via Route 29 Business. Parking spaces are abundant in the paved lot. The actual take out is on river right at Beaver Creek, which enters the James just upstream from Six-Mile Bridge. The put-in is down a short embankment, adjacent to State Route 726, which is off Route 460. Parking is very limited at roadside pull-offs. This is a non-trailerable site.

The Scotts Mill float begins in the heart of downtown Lynchburg. Across from the ramp on river right, you can see an old bridge support that spouts a fountain as well as various business buildings. And after launching, you can look upstream and espy Scotts Mill Dam and Route 29 Business. Perhaps the most interesting aspect of this float is that although it starts in the city and although city sounds are often in the background, the scenery is quite pleasing and wildlife, especially songbirds and waterfowl, is very abundant.

"I really like this float," says guide Jarod Harker of Confluence Outfitters. "After you float for a few minutes, you don't feel like you're in a city anymore. And there's some big smallmouths and muskies on this float."

The first hundred or so yards above and below the ramp is the haunt of muskie and catfish anglers, but soon the excellent smallmouth bass habitat that this trip is known for comes to the fore. The first major natural feature is Percival's Island, which is an exceptional birding area known for its warblers, vireos, and waterfowl. Be sure to take the left side of the island not only for superior angling but also because dam remains and a five-foot or so drop characterizes the right side. Tom Reisdorf, who is manager of Angler's Lane in nearby Forest and also a guide, relates that the brisk current along the river left bank draws smallies throughout the day. Like Harker, he feels that despite this trip beginning in Lynchburg, the junket quickly evolves into a rural getaway although city sounds are often in the background.

"The Scott's Mill float is fished a lot and is easy to access because of an excellent ramp," said Tom. "The trip also has all kinds of water: an easy Class I, lots of riffles, deep pools, water willow beds, and woody bank cover. People in the Lynchburg area especially will find it a great place to go after work."

Crankbaits and Clousers often produce well throughout the one-plus-mile that Percival's runs. Near the beginning of the float, you will also spot Route 29 crossing over the land mass. A railroad bridge marks the end of the island.

The James then makes a short river right turn that is marked by a sewage treatment fount entering the waterway. Eddies behind the discharge are worth checking out. The James then forms a river left bend that features numerous silver maples and box elders as well as scattered wood debris. The river also has a rocky bottom for much of this section, and the fishing can be quite good. Toward the end of the bend lies Setting Pole Falls, a misnomer for sure. Only in the spring is Setting Pole much of a falls and then it is just a Class I says Reisdorf. For much of the year, this is riffle water and the domain of active smallies.

The riffles continue as you drift by two islands. The best pathway is between the two of them, but you can scoot by on river left as well. This is yet

The Scotts Mill float begins in downtown Lynchburg.

another area where quality smallmouth sport can exist. The James then straightens and widens, and the fishing action slows. The Route 29 Bypass crosses the river and then the habitat begins to improve by the time Feagans Island, also known as Opossum Island, appears. It was in this area that I caught my first gar while on a junket with Reisdorf and Donna Honovi. Tom had earlier warned me that a school of gar, known for their prehistoric body traits of long tails, snout-like mouths, and ferocious-looking teeth, often finned this particular area.

I cast toward a water willow bed, and a gar rushed out toward the jerkbait and slashed at it, although futilely. The next cast caused another gar to wallop the lure with its tail, which resulted in the hook becoming embedded and the fish charging across the surface. I played the 18-inch fish for about a minute until I used a net to land it.

"Don't expect for me to hold that gar up for pictures," laughed Tom, which was a very understandable reaction. I used some needle-nosed pliers to dislodge the artificial, snapped some pictures of the gar within the net, and sent the fish on its way.

More excellent habitat exists above, within, and below Feagans Island. Not far downstream, you will need to maneuver over to river right where the Six Mile Bridge access point exists, upstream from the structure itself.

14 Six-Mile Bridge (Lynchburg) to Joshua Falls

TRIP: Six-Mile Bridge to Joshua Falls in Amherst and Campbell counties

USGS QUAD: Kelly

DISTANCE: Four miles

MAP: Page 110

RAPIDS: Several Class I rapids and riffles

ACCESS: The actual put-in is on river right at Beaver Creek, which enters the James just upstream from Six-Mile Bridge. The put-in is down a short embankment, adjacent to State Route 726, which is off Route 460. The river right take-out is off Route 726 via a gravel access road. The take-out is about 4,500 feet below Nine-Mile Bridge and about a mile above Joshua Falls. A boat slide leads to a concrete ramp.

Conventional wisdom is that quality outdoor recreation can't exist on this section because the trip practically begins in downtown Lynchburg. And besides, didn't this section suffer from water pollution in the past? Although the latter statement was once true, the water quality is now quite good on this section; and marvelous outdoor fun can take place in or near major Virginia cities such as Lynchburg.

Many years ago, I was introduced to the Six-Mile Bridge float by James Noel of Lynchburg. He rates this trek as one of the best on the entire upper river. I also recommend that you obtain a copy of The James River Batteau Festival Trail guide before beginning this or any other trip on the upper or middle river. I have seen no other map or guide that is so detailed concerning the rapids, islands, and hazards that dot the river. The map also gives information about the history of the bateaus and the epic adventures of the individuals who manned them in the 1800s. See Appendix for details on how to order the guide.

The first one and one-half miles or so of this float is straight, flat water. You will pass under Six-Mile Bridge and through a series of shallow riffles, none of which hold many quality fish. Then you will encounter the Buzzard Islands. I always find it interesting that even though the sights and sounds of Lynchburg are close, the river here can create the feeling that one is far away from civilization. I have caught some nice smallmouths from the Buzzard Islands area, and recall one particularly memorable trip where a two-pound smallmouth slashed across the water to slam a buzzbait. Fishermen should spend a great deal of time weaving in and out among the three major islands of this area. Cast to the downstream sides of the islands and to the eddies on all sides. The islands are also wonderful places to indulge in a short break and snap some photos. Look for great blue herons, belted kingfishers, and mallards.

After you paddle past the islands, you will encounter the beginning of a one and one-half mile long horseshoe bend on river left and then water willow beds and some extremely easy Class I rapids. This combination of water willow beds and current provides another good photo opportunity. Noel rates the fishing in this area as the best on the Six-Mile Bridge excursion, and I agree. Plan to spend at least ninety minutes or so here, and be sure to thoroughly probe the submerged wood cover. Hurl weedless three-inch grubs, six-inch worms, weighted nymphs, and streamers to these smallmouth hangouts. In fact, on one Six-Mile Bridge float, Noel and I both did well with fake crawlers. On that June day, we encountered several other fishermen who were experiencing a miserable time, catching only a few small fish. The gentlemen told us that they

A scenic view of the Six-Mile Bridge float.

were using crankbaits because the last time they had fished here those lures had engendered a number of strikes.

One of the aspects of angler behavior that always amazes me is how we are content to stay with the same old approach just because it worked previously. During a summer float, spin fishermen should have on hand at least five different categories of artificials: topwaters, soft plastics, jig-and-pigs, spinnerbaits, and crankbaits. Fly-fishermen should bring along their own quintet: poppers, hair bugs, streamers, nymphs, and damsel and dragon fly patterns. More and more, I prefer to tote both spin and fly tackle to increase my odds of success. If one lure or fly does not produce, I keep switching until I find something that works or until the trip ends. The fishermen we met that day were determined to "make" the bass bite crankbaits. The fish were not interested and the fishermen became frustrated. With experimentation, anglers can usually figure out what the bass are biting.

After the horseshoe bend terminates, you will encounter a series of riffles and then Nine-Mile Bridge. These riffles harbor plenty of smallmouths in the spring, and they are well worth the hard work. But by summer, the riffles have become only a few feet deep and the better fish have vacated them. This is a good example of how smallmouth haunts change with the seasons, and how fishermen also should take into account seasonal differences in bass habitat. Indeed, the only time that brown bass consistently appear in shallow one- to-two-foot deep riffles is during the spring season. The rest of the year, you are more likely to locate good-sized bass in water four feet deep or deeper.

Just one fishing area remains on this float, and it is only fair. Several hundred yards down from Nine-Mile Bridge lies a very short outside bend on river right. This turn does conceal some good fish in the spring, but again by summer the fish have moved on. Make a few quick casts to the downed wood along this shoreline and if no strikes occur, paddle through. The take-out is just downstream on river right, about a mile above Joshua Falls.

15 Joshua Falls to Riverville

TRIP: Joshua Falls to Riverville in Amherst, Campbell, Appomattox, and Nelson counties

USGS QUADS: Kelly, Stonewall, and Buffalo Ridge

DISTANCE: Sixteen Miles

MAP: Page 118

RAPIDS: The Class II Joshua Falls and Higginbothams Falls, numerous Class Is and riffles.

ACCESS: The put-in is on river right over a mile above Joshua Falls. (*See* gray box of the previous chapter.) A small community take-out exists near Riverville where Allens Creek enters on river left, just off Route 622. To take out, you will have to paddle under a stone tunnel/culvert over Allens Creek and haul your craft up a short, mud bank. Parking is just roadside pull-offs. This is a non-trailerable site.

The Joshua Falls float is a full-day one for floaters who can come close to journeying two miles an hour. If you are not a competent paddler in your craft of choice, then this is a junket that should not be taken. Float fishermen must employ a run-and-gun gameplan if they want to reach the take-out before dark, or gain permission from a local landowner to camp out along the river. Rob Campbell, Upper James River Outreach Coordinator for the James River Association, says his organization has long looked for access points in this section and will continue to do so in the coming years.

Several times I have asked landowners to let me camp out on the Joshua Falls excursion, and every time I have been granted permission. As a rural landowner myself, I am well-aware of how angry I can become when someone trespasses on my properties in Virginia and West Virginia. Without hesitation, I will call the Virginia Game Department or West Virginia DNR if I spot someone doing something illegally on my land. However, also as a rural landowner, I very much respect the individual who asks me for access, and I may or may not grant that request depending on a host of factors. When I am floating a long section like this one and decide that I can't continue for the day or make the take-out, I will look for a farmhouse along the river. I will admit to the landowner that I am tired and ask if that individual can help me out by granting permission to spend the night. I will promise not to litter or build a fire. Usually, folks are sympathetic to a direct, honest appeal and will help me out.

15

N

W — E

S

Scale in miles

0   1   2   3

Higgin

664

Wreck
Island
Creek

119

663

683

Wreck
Island

605

611

Riverville

600

825

832

623

605

Patterson
Shoals

704

667

Stonewall
Creek

776

624

608

Pettyjohn
Island

622

627

Earley Rd.

624

721

Chase
Island
Shoals

632

Partridge
Creek

Beck Creek

622

604

Joshua
Falls

609

Nine Mile
Bridge (Rail)

726

Joshua Falls Dam

Remains
of dam

Remains
of dam

Buzzard
Islands

Setting
Pole
Falls

672

Feagan's
Island

460

29

766

689

589

Creek

ek

The first half mile contains some rather flat, uninteresting water, which you may want to quickly paddle through, but then you'll come to a one-mile-long outside bend on river left. Scores of laydowns dot this bend, making it a prime place to work spinnerbaits and streamers.

Over halfway through the turn, Joshua Falls comes into view. The Joshua Falls Dam was built for the Kanawha Canal, and the remains of that dam serve as midstream obstructions today. Those remains create some white water hazards and some great fish-holding areas. The remnants also can cause a boat to broach if a paddler is careless. Indeed, this general area has always wreaked havoc with boats. During the early bateau days of the late 1700s and early 1800s, before the dam was constructed, there was a natural falls here. According to The James River Batteau Festival Trail guide, at this location several boats "have been wrecked & some lives lost." The bateau era is a fascinating one for history buffs and is a time period that many small towns along the upper and middle river now celebrate. Briefly, the main function of bateaux was to haul tobacco down river to Richmond. But the coming of the railroads doomed this form of commerce.

Today, the best path through Joshua Falls is right of center. This Class II rapid flaunts a number of mid-river boulders which can make for a tricky passage, especially on the left. Be sure to scout this rapid before running it. Active bass may be cruising here, so fishermen should get in a few casts to the upstream side of the rapid.

For several hundred yards below the falls, you'll find excellent fishing in the small eddies and rock-filled riffles. As you course through here, be sure to cast buzzbaits, grubs, and Sneaky Pete Poppers to the current breaks behind those obstructions. In fact, I recommend that after you make your initial pass through this section, you paddle upstream as far as possible and run this area again. Precious little decent fishing (and no exciting rapids) can be found throughout the remainder of this section. Next in view is a long, straight, rather monotonous stretch of one-half mile, and hard by that is an outside bend on river right that offers limited cover. The next mile is similarly uninteresting, offering nothing more than a shallow, straight expanse.

The rest of the Joshua Falls trek provides some of the most varied and enticing water on the upper river. For the no-nonsense river angler, this is a capital section that offers big bass potential. The next one and one-half mile of this float offers some nice scenery—tree-shrouded banks, gently flowing water, waterfowl, and occasional glimpses of ospreys and great blue herons. Although the vistas are appealing, anglers will find the fishing poor and white water fans will want to race through this section of the river.

The fishing is poor here because, as predators, gamefish such as small-mouth bass, muskie, and flathead catfish are creatures of the edge. That is, they prefer holding areas where two or more kinds of habitat merge. For example, brown bass will often lurk where a rock pile borders a water willow bed or a submerged log lies next to a boulder. This section offers very little edge habitat, and the bass have few places to congregate.

The Joshua Falls float is extremely long and meant for run and gun fishing.

The lack of edge habitat similarly causes this section to be uninspiring for white water seekers. Exciting water occurs where a change in the riverbed takes place. For instance, if the width of a stream suddenly narrows, water is forced through a more confined area. As a result, the water volume is forced to accelerate. Another example is where the stream bed takes a precipitous descent. Boulders tend to be found at such an area, and the combination of a drop and huge rocks creates white water.

A change in the river does happen when the Chase Island Shoals (a half-mile long cluster of three islands) comes into view. Go to the right of the first small island, and then to the left of the larger second island which appears next, and you will encounter the easiest passageway through these shoals and the best fishing. The water through this passage courses along fairly swiftly, making it fun—and easy—to run. During the summer, make quick casts toward the bank with a buzzbait or streamer to ascertain if bass are holding along the islands. Guide Tom Reisdorf, manager of the Angler's Lane in Forest, says that a blue popper is the gold standard on the Upper James.

"For summertime topwater fishing, few fly patterns are more consistently productive than a blue popper," he said. "Sometimes, the fish want it dead drifted, sometimes they want it popped, sometimes they want it in between."

Jared Harker, who operates Confluence Outfitters, acknowledges that summer is a great time for topwater action, but for overgrown smallies on the James, he prefers the late winter/early spring period.

"One of my favorite times of year to be on the river is from February through March," he said. "This two-month span produces some of the biggest and hardest fighting smallmouth of the entire year leaving little room for cabin fever. My favorite lure is a 2¾-inch black tube on a ¼-ounce jighead. I will cast it into deep, rocky pools and slow, deep water current seams. Retrieve the bait just slowly enough to avoid snags."

Some of the best shoreline cover on the entire middle river is on river left below the Chase Island Shoals. Lots of sycamores, silver maples, and downed timber can be found along the bank, as can plenty of rocky cover and water depths of between four and ten feet. This is jumbo smallmouth water! As such, I encourage you to tie on some known big-bass baits. Spinning rod fans should try one-half ounce jig-and-pigs, six-inch plastic worms and lizards, and one-fourth ounce buzzbaits. Fly-fishermen will want to cast Clouser Minnows and full-bodied hair bugs.

Once that bank cover concludes, though, so does the good fishing for the next two and one-half miles. The James becomes very straight, and paddlers and anglers will want to make short work of this stretch. No islands exist for travelers to eat a shore lunch or bird watch—another negative for this slow-moving portion. The excitement returns, however, with the advent of the half-mile-long or so Pettyjohn Island. The best route is to the right side of Pettyjohn. The water flows through here at a quick pace, making for a delightful change from the preceding section. This passageway is too shallow to hold fish except early and late in the day, so angling opportunities are limited.

Such is not the case as soon as you clear the island. A marvelous rocky shoreline rests on river right directly below the island's terminus, and I have landed some nice fish here that fell for Rebel Pop'Rs, one of the best topwater baits. Directly across the river lies a sandbar which announces the beginning of yet another splendid section—a laydown-strewn outside bend that goes on for over a half mile. It was here that I caught one of my nicest smallmouth bass ever from the upper James. I was paddling through this area on a foggy, summer morning when I spotted a bass marauding through a school of minnows. Those who do not spend much time outdoors sometimes perceive the natural world as being a placid place. In reality, nature—and the host of predators and prey that populate it—play out a life and death struggle every hour of every day.

The smallmouth bass was slashing through the shallows after the minnows in an attempt to engulf or to cripple and then consume as many as it could before the school dispersed. A situation such as this demands a buzzbait, so I hurled one into the hubbub. Predictably, the predator charged my bait and after a long and furious battle, I was able to bring the bass to boat. The smallmouth measured twenty inches, and I could have submitted the fish for a big fish citation from the state. But I recommend strict catch-and-release for larger smallmouths. Releasing fish is good for the environment—and for the soul. A stream smallmouth of that size may be ten or more years in age. By keeping it, I would have removed a superior fish from the gene pool and possibly denied another angler the joy of battling it. After I let the bass go, it charged back toward the bank—no doubt to shortly resume its never ending pursuit of prey.

After this outside bend ends, paddle quickly for a half mile until you reach Patterson's Shoals, another locale that bedeviled the bateau men of the 1700s and 1800s. The left bank through the shoals is featureless, but the right contains a great deal of wood and rock cover. This is another hot spot on this trek. A short distance below Patterson's Shoals, you may be able to catch a glimpse of a scout totem pole on river left. The pole is much more visible in the spring and fall than in summer's heavy foliage.

Directly downstream from the totem pole is Christian Island; go to the river left side of the island and employ crankbaits and weighted nymphs to prospect the cover to your right. You should encounter no difficulty through this passageway unless the river is high. Wreck Island soon materializes and the good fishing returns. One of the better feeding flats on the middle river exists above and to the right of Wreck Island. This particular flat, which is characterized by a number of large rocks in three to five feet of water, serves as a destination for smallmouths when they leave the main channel and move shallow to forage.

Bronzebacks can do so at any time of the day or night, which explains why sometimes feeding flats such as this one brim with fish and at other times they will be totally barren of activity. The head of Wreck Island is a fine spot to take a break and eat lunch. Some fetching scenery can be glimpsed on river right, and I like to take photos of that view. Wreck Island and its adjacent rocky bottom extends for nearly a mile and was another site that often caused bateau men to lose their cargo and sometimes their lives.

Some marvelous fishing can be found between Joshua Falls and Riverville.

Soon after you take the river left channel by Wreck Island, you will encounter Wreck Island Falls. A drop of five feet causes some fairly strong Class I rapids and riffles in this 300-yard-long section. The passageway is fairly narrow and rocky, so canoeists should pay strict attention. Once you are below the falls, pivot the canoe and paddle back upstream until you eddy out in the pool directly below the end of the falls. I often deploy a boat in this manner so that I can work a pool below a riffle or rapid. This type of place can be one of the most productive on any river.

The next mile or so of the James is easy to navigate. Riverville Falls lies at the beginning of this section, but it is nothing more than a riffle or weak Class I. The best route is to far river left. Riverville Falls is followed by an outside bend on river left that provides mediocre fishing at best. This bend is void of the cover that is found on many other curves in the river.

For white water lovers, the best part of the Joshua Falls trip comes last— the infamous Higginbothams Falls. On my first charge through this Class II, my friend James Noel and I did just about everything wrong—and just by random chance managed not to tip over his canoe. The best passageway is on the right side of a small island that divides the falls. We, however, took the left route and almost slammed head-on into a boulder. That near disaster could have been avoided if we had not had so much difficulty making up our minds concerning which route to take—indecision is a cardinal sin for any river runner. In our case, the boat was captured by the current before we had decided on our route. Regardless of which path you select, this strong Class II requires that you scout it thoroughly before attempting a run. In fact, if you are unsure of your canoeing skills, this rapid is one that you might want to portage. When water levels are low, you may be able to paddle a canoe up to the small island, drag the craft across the island, and avoid the falls altogether.

After Higginbothams Falls, less than a mile remains on this float and it is unremarkable. The take-out is where Allens Creek enters on river left. You will have to paddle up this creek a short distance, pass under a culvert, and then haul your craft up a mud bank to your right. For the most part, though, the Joshua Falls trip makes for a wonderful day on the James.

16 Riverville to Bent Creek

TRIP: Riverville to Bent Creek in Nelson and Appomattox counties

USGS QUADS: Buffalo Ridge and Gladstone

DISTANCE: Two and one-half miles

MAP: Page 126

RAPIDS: Numerous riffles

ACCESS: The put-in is where Allens Creek enters on river left, just off Route 622. (See gray box of the previous chapter for details.) The take-out is on river right at Bent Creek where the Route 60 Bridge crosses the river. The ramp is concrete and parking is available in a gravel lot. Unloading from a trailer may be difficult in low water.

At first glance, the Riverville trip may seem too short to be significant. For the individual interested only in canoeing, such is probably the case, and that person perhaps should combine this trip with the Bent Creek float. However, the nature lover, photographer, and angler can easily spend a half day on this two and one-half mile section of the river.

After the put-in, the beginning of Smith Islands appears, and these islands will dominate most of the rest of the trip. Right above the islands, scattered rocks speckle the left shoreline, and anglers should find topwaters such as Heddon Tiny Torpedos, Sneaky Pete Poppers, Phillips Crippled Killers, and Rebel Pop'Rs effective. The Tiny Torpedo and Sneaky Pete have long been popular topwaters on America's smallmouth rivers, but the Crippled Killer and Pop'R were famed a generation ago and only recently made a comeback. I have always been amazed at how fickle the angling public is when it comes to buying lures and flies. The hot new fish catcher one season finds itself at the bottom of the tacklebox the next, replaced by another with a similarly brief time in the sun. Actually, the Crippled Killer and Pop'R never stopped being attractive to fish, only to fishermen.

Another reason to tote along a variety of topwater lures and flies for warm water fishing is that the fish truly do prefer one over another on some days. For example, I have seen days when the bronzebacks wanted only the "swoosh, swoosh" of the Tiny Torpedo in the mornings, the "pop, spit" of the Pop'R in the afternoons, the "swish, swish" of the Crippled Killer in the evenings, or the "pop, pop" of a Sneaky Pete at twilight. Other days the fish

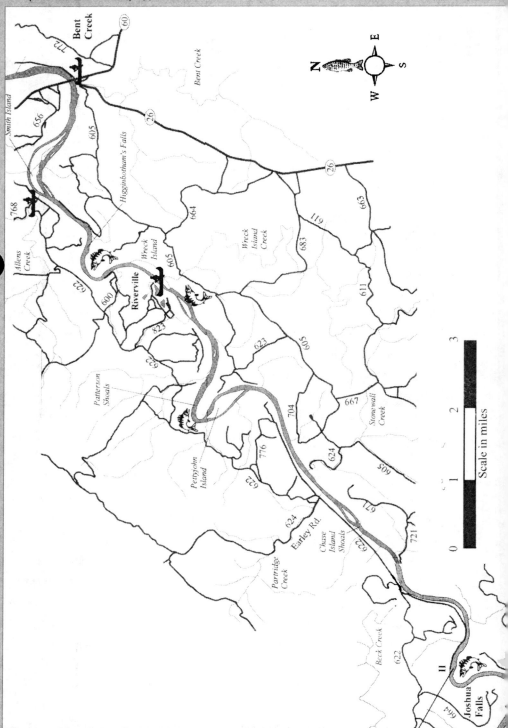

solely desire the churning rhythm of buzzbaits or the shimmying of a hair bug at rest. And of course there are days when any or none of these offerings work. I cannot explain why this is so, it simply is.

Smith Islands is a mecca for shorebirds and waterfowl, and the wildlife photographer and bird watcher will want to have a camera, binoculars, and field guides handy. Expect to see great blue herons, green herons, belted king-fishers, mallards, and maybe even wood ducks and ospreys. In addition to the wildlife, the islands themselves make for fetching scenic shots. I like to frame my shots so that I include island, sky, and river in equal proportions.

Primitive canoe-in camping is allowed on the island chain which is privately owned. (No facilities exist, so please be careful not to litter and to leave the islands as you found them.) If a canoeist is on a multiple-day float trip, the islands are an especially pleasant place to spend a night. Be sure to set up your tent well away from the water. Once on a trip to the Rapidan River, a friend and I erected our tent too close to the stream. A thunderstorm beat down on the area over night, and we awoke around 3:00 a.m. with the water lapping at the sides of the tent. We were quite unnerved and disoriented when this

The James has a mixture of deep water and riffles between Riverville and Bent Creek.

happened, and it is an experience I do not wish to have again.

For the Smith Islands, take the left channel throughout its one and one-half-mile length. Cast to the river left bank or the islands themselves as you search for pocket water. At some places, you will encounter water four or more feet deep and at other places the depth is less than a foot. At the end of the main body of islands, a number of islets exist. Most are heavily populated with vegetation and lie in water six or more feet deep. I have found these small islands to consistently draw more fish than the main chain upstream. Work the downstream sides of these islets with crayfish patterns, six-inch plastic worms, four-inch craw worms, and jig-and-pigs. On one trip to the Smith Islands, a friend and I witnessed the value of bringing along more than one fishing rod per person. The handle of one of my friend's spinning reels fell off near one of the islets, and he spent a fruitless half hour trying to dive and recover it. Fortunately, he had several other outfits in the canoe and could continue fishing.

I always bring at least three or four outfits on any excursion, sometimes I carry five, and I have a good friend who insists he needs seven. River fishermen are much more sophisticated than they used to be and now realize that one rod just can not do the job nor is it prudent to have one outfit, especially if something goes wrong with it. For example, a typical lineup is a medium spinning rod for topwater baits, a medium spinning rod for crankbaits, a medium heavy spinning rod for plastic worms, a medium heavy baitcaster for jig-and-pigs, and a nine-foot, eight-weight fly rod with sinking tip and floating lines. Each outfit is particularly well suited for a particular offering, but won't work well at all for another. Sometimes the fly rod will outperform the spinning and baitcasting outfits, especially those warm, sunny days when the bass engulf aquatic insects on top. And sometimes only the spinfishing or baitcasting rods will produce, especially if the bass are hugging the bottom in deep water. Rod selection should be based on what kind of natural forage the fish are likely to be consuming at a particular time of the year, and the water depth the bass are holding.

The next one-half mile or so of this float is fairly straight and the fishing is poor. But the three-hundred yards above the Bent Creek take-out offers some of the best deep water ledge habitat I have found anywhere on any river. Boulders, logs, and brush litter the pool, much of it over ten feet deep. I have spent as long as ninety minutes in this section; cast deep running crankbaits, jig-and-pigs, plastic worms, and weighted streamers and crawfish patterns to the submerged cover. The months of March and April are prime to work this section because trophy smallmouths will gang up in this form of habitat at that time. Some jumbo smallmouths spend the entire year—and their entire lives—in this type of environment.

The U.S. Route 60 Bridge helps mark this section, and the short but eventful Riverville journey.

17 Bent Creek to Wingina

TRIP: Bent Creek to Wingina in Nelson, Appomattox, and Buckingham counties

USGS QUADS: Gladstone, Shipman, and Howardsville

DISTANCE: Twelve and one-half miles

MAP: Page 130

RAPIDS: Several Class I rapids, plenty of riffles

ACCESS: The put-in is on river right at Bent Creek where the Route 60 Bridge crosses the river. The ramp is concrete and parking is available in a gravel lot. Unloading from a trailer may be difficult in low water. The concrete ramp take-out is on river left at Wingina where the Route 56 Bridge crosses. Parking is available in a gravel lot. Steep dropoff at end of ramp and current can make unloading difficult.

The Bent Creek to Wingina trek is one of the longer trips on the James and one of the better known floats in the state. Because of its popularity, this section receives quite a bit of angling and canoeing pressure. Anglers will have to know where the best spots are in order to maximize their time on the water. Canoeists should allot five to seven hours, while anglers will need eight to ten hours.

Immediately below the put-in at the Route 60 Bridge, paddle through the first long shallow stretch of about one-half mile. Doing so is often difficult for many individuals because they have a tendency to want to fish hard at the start of a trip. But this float is so long that you simply cannot waste time on unproductive areas and still have time to hit the highlights.

Freeland's Falls is the next focal point. This area, which consists of nearly a half mile of riffles and an easy Class I, is too shallow for most of the year to consistently hold quality mossybacks and other gamefish. Only during the spring period does Freeland's Falls offer much potential—and it is limited even then. The river next forms an inverted S-curve over the next one and one-half miles. The first sector of the curve provides some adequate wood cover on river left, but the remainder of this area is quite void of fish-holding structure. Almost always, bends on the James excel as fish producers, but such is not the case here.

Another anomaly occurs on the following one-mile-long straight section. Usually, extended straight sections of the James are shallow and featureless. This part of the Bent Creek trip, however, contains some excellent mid-river dropoffs

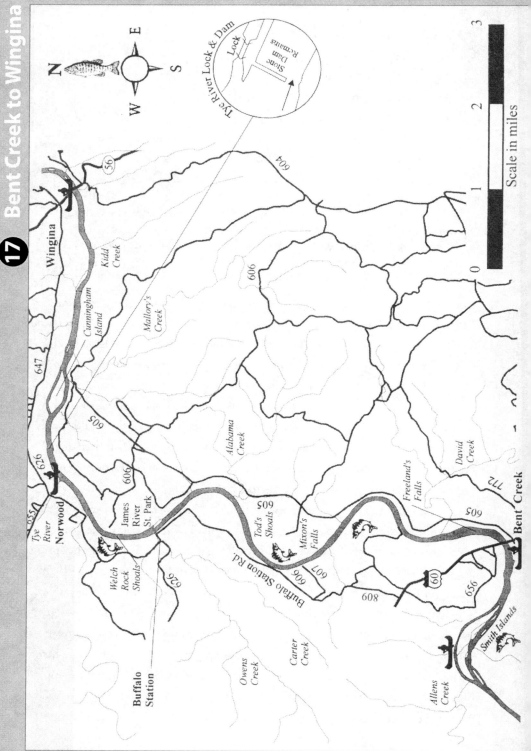

17 Bent Creek to Wingina

Tye River Lock & Dam

Lock

Stone Dam Remains

Scale in miles

0 1 2 3

Wingina

Kidd Creek

Cunningham Island

Mallory's Creek

647

605

606

626

Tye River

Norwood

James River St. Park

Welch Rock Shoals

Buffalo Station

Owens Creek

Carter Creek

Alabama Creek

Buffalo Station Rd.

Tod's Shoals

Mixon's Falls

Freeland's Falls

David Creek

605

606

607

608

605

772

60

656

Allens Creek

Smith Islands

Bent Creek

56

604

606

in eight to ten feet of water. Even if time is limited—as indeed it may be on such a long float—I recommend that you budget your time so that you spend a great deal of it here. On one journey through this deep water haven, I picked up some nice smallies that hit crawfish imitations.

Mixon's Falls, the next landmark, is a very easy Class I rapid which is intermixed with riffles. Then comes one of the better fishing spots on the Bent Creek trip—the Tod's Shoals area. The outside bend on river left that precedes Tod's Shoals features lots of my favorite kind of bank cover: sycamores. Wherever you fish on the James, you can just about count on a sycamore-shrouded bank to harbor gamefish. The extensive root system and the trees themselves when they topple into the river create plenty of hiding places for bass and their prey. Try Dahlburg Divers, hair bugs, and Texas-rigged grubs, tube baits, and spider jigs here. Tod's Shoals itself contains basketball-sized underwater rocks for some 100 yards. This is the type of area where, for several reasons, I can easily spend an hour. First, smallmouths in deep water rock habitat live here throughout much of the year. The angler can be assured that if he makes the proper presentation with the correct lure or fly, he will catch fish. Second, determining the correct offering can take consider-able time. The individual who "runs and guns" through water like Tod's Shoals has very little chance of determining a pattern.

A sound approach, then, is to begin casting with lures of flies that can be retrieved very quickly, and then progressively turn to slower moving baits. For instance, I like to fan-cast an area like Tod's Shoals with streamers or spinner-baits and crankbaits when I first arrive. If these fail, then I toss topwaters such as Sneaky Petes, Tiny Torpedos, Pop'Rs, and Storm Chug Bugs. The latter lure, with its rattle chamber, is especially productive if the water is stained or cloudy. Finally, I slow down and inch along Woolly Buggers, hellgrammite patterns or worms, lizards, and grubs. And by all means, try big bass baits such as Clouser Minnows and jig-and-pigs before you leave a rocky pool.

With a few exceptions, the bass fishing is quite mediocre for the next three miles. While run-and-gun fishing is unwise through Tod's Shoals, it is the solution through here. Fan-cast the shallow Bork's Shoals area, which lies on a river right outside bend a mile into this section, with streamers and medium running crankbaits and then move on. Approximately a half mile downstream, where Route 606 parallels the stream, comes a series of dropoffs along the river left shoreline. Cast crawfish imitations to these areas to ascertain if any bass are at home.

You then reach, on river left, the Buffalo Station area, which is roughly half way through the Bent Creek float. Across from Buffalo Station is the James River State Park. Fields dot the shoreline of this section, and in the morning and evening paddlers can expect to glimpse deer feeding in these openings. Waterfowl also tend to congregate here. River runners should note that two alternative access points exist at the state park on river right. However, you must pay a fee if you use the park's access points or parking areas. The upstream ramp is called Canoe Landing and occurs about half way through the float. As its name indicates, this is a canoe or kayak launch and is not suited for motorized boats. The second access point, Dixon Landing, is a concrete ramp and is suited for small boats. This access point is about two miles downstream from Canoe Landing.

Angling opportunities are quite limited, though, and I recommend a fifteen-minute or so paddle to reach the Welch Rock Shoals area. This is one of the best sections on the upper river with the numerous riffles a key to this topflight action. On my initial trip through this area, a light fog enveloped the river and I observed smallmouths feeding heavily. Hordes of bass chased schools of minnows across the surface, and the excitement and action overwhelmed my senses. There is something special about fishing in fog—it seems to bring out the inherent wildness in a river. I must caution, though, that if fog becomes too dense, you should beach your craft and wait for visibility to improve. Floating down any river when conditions prevent you from seeing more than a few feet ahead is extremely dangerous.

A number of huge rocks dot Welch Rock Shoals. One boulder in particular is worth noting. It is roughly the size of a small truck, and this structure resides about fifteen yards from the river left bank. A side current courses between the rock and shoreline, and trees form a canopy along the slightly undercut bank. This location shouts smallmouth, and I like to work it for some twenty minutes. The shoals proper also contain a number of current breaks and dropoffs and are well worth your time.

The entrance of the Tye River on river left is the next major landmark. Smallmouths populate the last fifteen or so miles of the Tye, a very underrated waterway. However, it's very silted where the Tye commingles with the James, and you should make haste through it. Below the merging of the rivers, look for the remains of the Tye River Dam and, several hundred yards later, a ledge that runs across the river. Solid smallmouth sport takes place below both of these obstructions. Of the two, I prefer the ledge. Cast topwaters to the base of the ledge and work them rapidly. A deep water pool follows hard on to the ledge and is an excellent place to cast weighted streamers and Carolina-rigged craw worms and lizards. Of historical note is that at the ledge, the remains of a bateau sluice lie adjacent to the river right bank. Sluices were cut into the river bottom so that boats could more easily pass through on their way to Richmond. Sometimes, however, debris filled the sluices, creating one more hazard for an already dangerous trip down the James.

About one-quarter mile below the ledge is a river right shoreline replete with rock and wood cover. If you are a canoeist, this is a good spot to eddy out and take a meal break. Fishermen will want to probe the underwater cover in this area. Paddle for about five minutes and you will reach Cunningham Island, also known as Helena's Island. The Nature Conservancy owns this wildlife haven. One of the Nature Conservancy's major goals is to protect and preserve wildlife habitat—an objective that all those who love nature should be able to share. I often worry about the feuding that takes place among anglers and non-anglers, hunters and non-hunters, and conservationists and preservationists. Surely, we should all be able to agree that the protection of wildlife habitat is something that is a necessity, especially with the world's rapidly expanding human population. The Nature Conservancy should be supported by outdoor lovers of all persuasions.

Cunningham Island splits the river, and the island can be run from either side. The next two miles are, for the most part, very shallow and have a pebble bottom. I recommend a quick paddle to the river left take-out at Wingina below the Route 56 Bridge.

18 **19**

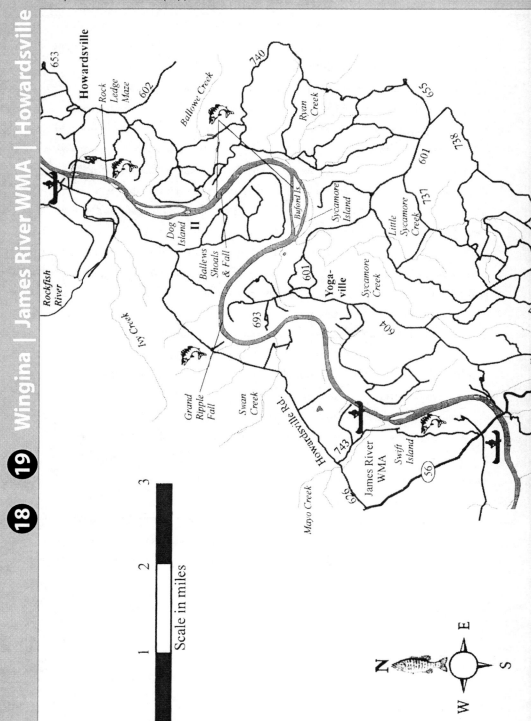

Scale in miles
0 1 2 3

⓲ Wingina to James River Wildlife Management Area

> **TRIP:** Wingina to James River Wildlife Management Area (WMA) in Nelson and Buckingham counties
>
> **USGS QUAD:** Howardsville
>
> **DISTANCE:** Two and one-half miles
>
> **MAP:** Opposite, page 134
>
> **RAPIDS:** Several Class I rapids and riffles
>
> **ACCESS:** The concrete ramp put-in is on river left at Wingina where the Route 56 Bridge crosses. Parking is available in a gravel lot. Steep dropoff at end of ramp and current can make unloading difficult. The take-out is on river left at the James River WMA, located off Route 626. The ramp is concrete, and parking is available.

Although the Wingina outing is a very short one, float fishermen can easily spend a good five hours checking out a number of areas. Canoeists, however, can just as easily whiz through here in an hour or two and might combine this trip with the James River WMA to Howardsville float.

Directly below the put-in, water willow islets speckle the river for a hundred yards or so. If you arrive at the James at first light, these islets are super places to utilize top-waters. At any time of the day, wade fishermen can enjoy some sport in this area. Another likely spot lies about half a mile below the bridge. After a straight stretch that is void of cover, you come to a long deep pool with a series of dropoffs and a sycamore-lined bank on river right. On one trip through here, I scored with Texas-rigged plastic crawfish in pumpkin-pepper that were bumped across some superlative rocky cover. This brings us to three relevant points concerning fishing crayfish imitations on the James.

First, I believe that smallmouths strike many lures or files out of reflex—something darts by and they instinctively slash at it. Crankbaits and streamers are prime examples of baits that elicit this behavior. On the other hand, bogus crawdads are "fool 'em" baits. I believe that bass think these fake crustaceans are the real thing, and when they move toward the bait, they fully intend to consume it. The majority of mud bugs that dwell in the James sport a distinct yellowish-brown color. Lure manufacturers concoct many hues that duplicate this color, among them pumpkinseed, pumpkin-pepper, butterscotch, and green pumpkin. However, I must confess that I now believe that of all the many factors that may cause a black bass to bite a lure, color is the least important. In fact, I believe that anglers, both spin and fly fishermen, waste too much time agonizing about what is the best and/or hot color for the fish on a certain waterway. I had much rather a lure or fly moves like something that a bass would want to eat rather than looks like something a bass does eat.

Second, as noted above, I recommend that you try to retrieve imitations in a way that simulates the movements of real crawfish. For example, too many people retrieve fake 'dads by dragging them across the bottom. To maximize the potential of a lure or pattern, retrieve it in short hops across the substrate; in other words, make it move like the real thing.

Third, if you are a spin fisherman, use sliding

Always pause for a few seconds to cast to water willow.

bullet sinkers that match the depth and current flow of the water you are fishing. Too many anglers will affix a certain size sinker to their line and leave it on all day. The result is that if the sinker is too light, the bait never descends to the bottom and is well out of a bass's strike zone. Or if the sinker is too heavy, the artificial constantly snags on the bottom. The following is a good formula for weight sizes: for spooky bass in shallow, still, or very clear water use one-eighth-ounce sliding bullet sinkers; for bass in moderately flowing water use quarter- to three-eighths-ounce weights; for fish in swiftly flowing current use one half- to three-quarter-ounce weights. Of course, there are many exceptions, so remember to experiment with weight sizes if strikes do not occur regularly. Fly-fishermen should employ sinking tip lines and, if necessary, split shot. I personally dislike the aesthetics of affixing shot above a crawfish pattern, but sometimes doing so is necessary to enable it to descend deeply enough. Last, tie on crawfish baits and patterns that have a lifelike texture and shape. Again, these traits are more important in a lure than its color. For fly patterns, consider those that bear the names of Dahlberg, Clouser, and Whitlock.

Only one tiptop fishing area remains on this short jaunt, and it comes one and one-half miles into the Wingina float: the area immediately above Swift Island and the entire river left route by the island. For fishermen, canoeists, and nature lovers, Swift is a pleasure! Vegetation flourishes on the island and it is a haven for vireos, warblers, waterfowl, herons, and kingfishers. It is also a fantastic spot to stop for a shore lunch and take pictures. Since the Wingina float is so brief, Swift Island is an ideal place for the shutterbug to revel in nature.

Canoeists will enjoy the delightfully brisk pace that the river takes. Class I rapids and riffles exist throughout, and they also have an upside for anglers. The well-aerated water results in actively feeding bass during the summer, and I have caught some quality fish here even during the dog days of August. As is the norm for fast water situations, anglers should offer baits that can be retrieved quickly, such as streamers, buzzbaits, spinnerbaits, crankbaits, and that old river standard: grubs on jig heads.

The last half mile or so is nothing more than a rather bland stretch of bank and bottom that brings you to the James River WMA public boat landing on river left. The Wingina float may be short in length, but it is long on fun.

19 James River WMA to Howardsville

TRIP: James River Wildlife Management Area to Howardsville in Nelson, Buckingham, and Albemarle counties

USGS QUAD: Howardsville

DISTANCE: Ten miles

MAP: Page 134

RAPIDS: Two Class II and several Class I rapids, and numerous riffles

ACCESS: The put-in is on river left at the James River WMA, located off Route 626. The ramp is concrete, and parking is available. The take-out is on river left, immediately below the mouth of the Rockfish River and just off Route 626. The ramp is privately owned and operated by Howardsville Canoe Livery (www.HowardsvilleCanoe.com). There is a drop box in the parking lot for accepting cash only payment.

The canoeist who is also a photographer will want to take the James River WMA trek in October after the leaves turn. A nice mixture of fields and wooded shorelines characterize this float, and the maples, sycamores, and other trees sport fall foliage that is truly inspiring. Paddlers can easily scoot through this section in four to five hours, but they may want to allot more time just to enjoy the scenery.

Float fishermen should consider this a day trip. On my visits here I have found that I needed about seven hours to work it thoroughly. The first two miles of this outing has very few fishing opportunities, so I recommend paddling until you arrive at a mile-long outside bend on river left. The area you skip is known as Yogaville, and the water here is very flat, deep, and featureless, however the outside bend initiates some stupendous fishing. Look for a series of laydowns, undercut banks, and even one section that has some standing dead trees in deep water. This is one of the few places on the entire upper river that contains this type of fish habitat.

On an early October excursion through here, a friend and I landed smallies up to two pounds. The fish hit Bill Lewis Rat-L-Tops, a noisy topwater prop bait. The tail end of October is about the latest fishermen can expect to experience surface action. By November, the fish have largely departed from the riffles and eddies and taken up residence in deeper pools until early spring. For the cooler water, tie on Woolly Buggers, jig-and-pigs, craw worms, and half-ounce spinner-baits. Retrieve these baits slowly.

Grand Ripple Falls looms just over half way through the bend. These falls are really nothing more than a riffle area, and they tend to concentrate smallmouths. They are also an excellent blend of current, deep water, and rocky habitat. I like to beach my canoe and wade upstream from the falls. Some water willow beds add to the area's appeal.

Right below Grand Ripple Falls, I once had the pleasure of observing a flock of wild turkeys feeding along the shoreline. Several birds even took flight and crossed the river. The wild turkey is my favorite bird and, tragically, it was almost eradicated from the Old Dominion earlier in this century. Through hunting license fees, habitat restoration, and other efforts by groups like the National Wild Turkey Federation of which I am a member, sportsman and conservation groups brought this game bird back. Today, well over 100,000 wild turkeys dwell in Virginia. On that particular trip, I must have seen some three dozen turkeys.

You will have to paddle about one and one-half miles to come to another potential hot spot. Next you'll find Sycamore Island on river right and Buford Island on the left, which together cover nearly a mile of river. Go to the left of Buford Island in order to explore some deep water riffles and rocky cover. Canoeists will enjoy the fast pace at which these riffles carry them along while anglers will want to retrieve streamers, crankbaits, and grubs around the many underwater rocks that stud this section. I have battled some nice fish here that charged out from behind rocks to "kiss" a lure or fly.

After Buford Island, paddle a little over a mile until you reach Ballews Shoals and Fall. Ballews shields perhaps the best underwater rocky cover on the James River WMA float, and I like to spend at least a half hour here. This is a wonderful place to toss crayfish imitations. Tom Stanley, an avid angler from Cumberland County, likes to employ live 'dads in this area. Tom rigs this bait with a light wire hook and with split shot placed about 18 inches up the line. On one trip through here, Stanley thoroughly out-fished me with live crayfish while I stubbornly stuck to artificials. On some days when the fish are inactive, live bait is just about the only way to entice bronzebacks. A Class I to II rapid (depending on water levels) concludes the Ballews' section—run it on far river left.

Two other nice areas remain. Just below Ballews Shoals and Fall lies Dog Island. At its beginning, Dog Island flaunts a very challenging Class II rapid, especially in the spring or during high water conditions anytime. Take the right channel when you come to the head of Dog Island. Next, turn right and then make a sharp left to weave your way through some boulders and reach a safe channel on the right. This maneuver must be executed fairly quickly if you are to slide through this rocky locale successfully. I recommend scouting this area beforehand. If you have any doubts about your paddling skills, debark at Dog Island and tote your craft around this rapid. Once you make it past the head of this island, some fetching rocky cover characterizes the rest of the passage. Also of note are some downed trees that litter the river right bank.

The Howardsville trip is very popular.

Less than a half mile below Dog Island, Rock Ledge Maze appears. This is a very descriptive place name for a portion of the James River WMA float that is just chock full of smallmouths. The "maze" consists of very large boulders and very small islands covered with water willow. Even though I am often tired by the time I arrive at this section, I like to spend at least an hour here casting topwaters to the many structures.

Rock Ledge Maze is also a delightful place to enjoy as you have lunch or take pictures. I like to set up on a rock and use the downstream boulders to frame my shots. When capturing the hues of autumn is my objective, I prefer a 28mm lens. When the objective is a close-up of a fish or a smallmouth with a fly in its mouth, a macro lens is the choice. My camera and fishing license goin a lunch box-sized Pelican case, enabling me to travel light. Of course, no photographer should venture forth on a river without a camera case that is both water and shock proof.

After Rock Ledge Maze, the remaining mile or so of the James River WMA float provides only marginal fishing and no challenging rapids. The Route 602 Bridge in the distance announces the beginning of the end of this trip. Soon after, you will note where the Rockfish River enters on river left; a few yards below that the Howardsville ramp appears on the same side. During the warm water period, expect to see a number of swimmers and tubers lolling about in the ramp area. And no wonder — the James River WMA to Howardsville section truly has something for everyone.

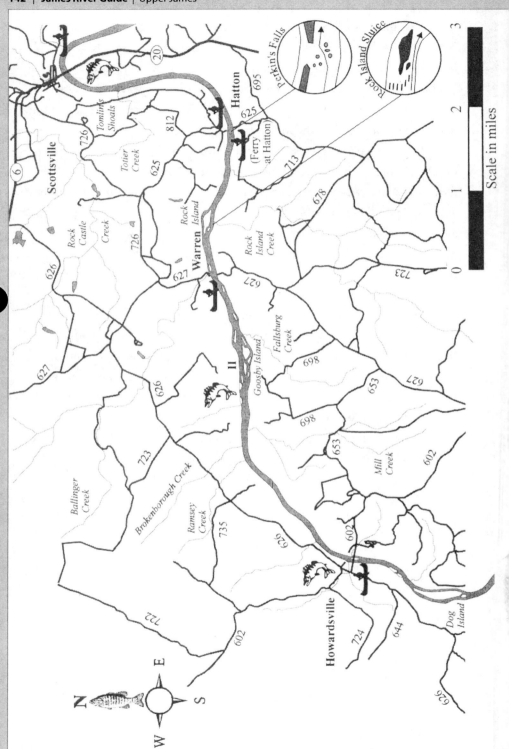

Scale in miles

Pelkin's Falls

Rock Island Sluice

Scottsville

Tomlin's Shoals

726

812

625

Totier Creek

Hatton

695

625

(Ferry at Hatton)

713

678

Rock Island Creek

Rock Island

726

Warren

627

627

Rock Castle Creek

626

723

627

626

Fallsburg Creek

Goosby Island

698

723

653

627

698

653

Ballinger Creek

723

Brokenborough Creek

Ramsey Creek

735

626

Mill Creek

602

602

722

602

Howardsville

724

644

Dog Island

626

N
E
S
W

20 Howardsville to Scottsville

TRIP: Howardsville to Scottsville in Albemarle, Buckingham, and Fluvanna counties

USGS QUADS: Howardsville, Glenmore, Esmont, and Scottsville

DISTANCE: Eleven miles

MAP: Opposite, page 142

RAPIDS: A number of Class I and Class II rapids, and riffles

ACCESS: The put-in is on river left, immediately below the mouth of the Rockfish River and just off Route 626. The ramp is privately owned and operated by Howardsville Canoe Livery (.www.HowardsvilleCanoe.com). There is a drop box in the parking lot for accepting cash only payment. The take-out is on river left, located just downstream from the Route 20 Bridge and just off Route 6. The ramp is concrete and parking is available.

The Howardsville float lacks excitement at its beginning and end, but the middle portion of this getaway has much to recommend it. Paddlers can easily cover this section in four to six hours while fishermen should figure on eight or nine hours if they want to work the best stretches thoroughly.

My initial voyage on the Howardsville section gave me insight on how to catch fish in muddy water. The time was mid-June, and the river was still high and discolored from late spring downpours. Right after the put-in, a series of ledges cross the James, forming riffles and some dropoffs. I knew that this area was the only place in the first three miles or so that had the reputation for producing good bass. My boatmate and I decided to commit ourselves to finding a pattern. After a great deal of experimentation, we determined that the smallmouths would hit spinnerbaits inched along the bottom. Ever since that day, my "go-to" bait for muddy water mossybacks has been this blade bait. But be forewarned: make-up of this artificial is crucial.

First, the blades should emit considerable vibration. Colorado blades are best for this purpose. These round blades do not give off the flash of willowleaf blades (which are long and thin), but flash is almost nonexistent in stained water anyway. The "thumping" of two Colorado blades produces sounds that bass can key in on. Second, the skirt for the spinnerbait should be chartreuse. This color is relatively visible in muddy water and gives fish something else to arouse their predatory instinct. Chartreuse also matches the green hues of many

The islands between Howardsville and Scottsville often provide good fishing.

minnows that inhabit the river. Last, spinnerbaits should be retrieved slowly in muddy liquid. Bass need extra time to locate lures then and slower retrieves allow this to happen. Smallmouths also hold in predictable places during high, muddy water. Look for them to be in cuts along the bank if the water is rising. If the water is dropping, the fish will relocate to midstream ledges, as was the case on my trip.

After the series of ledges, paddle three miles or so until you arrive at Goosby Island and the many miniature islets above and below it. Fishing can be outstanding on all sides of these islands. Target the shallower upstream sides with hair bugs, prop baits, and shallow-running crankbaits and streamers. Work the deeper downstream sides with spinnerbaits, weighted Clouser Minnows, and medium-running crankbaits. When the time comes to run Goosby Island, paddlers and float fishermen may want to take different routes. White water fans will probably desire the far river left route which involves Class II rapids, standing waves, and a rock garden. Some adroit maneuvering is necessary; expect to take on some water. Anglers should definitely select the river right route. Retrieve streamers, hellgrammite nymphs, and grubs through the Class I rapids and riffles on this side. A point forms at the end of the island; I once took a fine two-pound smallmouth here on a spinnerbait. This area is extremely scenic because of the numerous islets, wooded shorelines, and swift water. Shutterbugs will definitely want to beach their craft just below the island in order to compose some scenics.

Below Goosby Island comes a number of small islands and Class I rapids. This area is also superb for smallmouths, and you will want to cast some fast-moving flies and lures that imitate dace and other minnows. In fact, I would rate the Goosby Island area as your most likely place to catch a three-pound-plus bass on the Howardsville float. Allot a minimum of two hours here. When it comes to designating angling time for the James, my philosophy is to stroke like mad through the "dead water," then to camp out on the "hot spots."

After you pass the islets below Goosby, paddle a mile to Warren. An old cable passes over the river, indicating that this was once a ferry crossing. Less than a mile below Warren, another very panoramic area comes into sight. A series of bluffs line the river right bank, followed by riffles, and Little Rock and Rock islands. When I first glimpsed these bluffs, I immediately beached the canoe in order to take some photos. The islands are incredibly photogenic, particularly on a day when the sky is blue, as it was on that trip. After snapping some pictures, take the far river right route by the two islands. The riffles through here often hold active fish, so this is another section that calls out for quickly retrieved artificials.

Another mile or so will bring you to the Hatton Ferry Crossing at the end of Route 625 on river left. I highly recommend James River Runners, operated by Jeff and Christine Schmick, for quality canoe trips on the upper river. Just opposite James River Runners is Perkins Falls, a Class I to II rapid. Take the left-of-center passage, and be sure to work the pool below Perkins. Only three miles or so now remain of the Howardsville float, and fishing is only fair, with one exception. A little over two miles below Hatton Ferry, Tomlin's Shoals comes into view. This rock-laden area concentrates solid numbers of bass, especially in the spring. If your time has become limited by this stage of the float, you will still want to check this area before paddling out. The last mile or so of the trip features slow, deep water and is not especially noteworthy for the angler or paddler.

The Scottsville ramp not only heralds the end of the Howardsville float, but also the terminus of the upper James. Before leaving the area, take time to soak in the local color of Scottsville: a charming, old river town replete with stores, restaurants, bed and breakfasts, and a museum.

Middle James

21 Scottsville to Hardware River WMA 148

22 Hardware River WMA to Bremo Bluff 153

23 Bremo Bluff to Columbia 158

24 Columbia to Cartersville 163

25 Cartersville to West View 167

26 West View to Maidens 170

27 Maidens to Watkins Landing 174

28 Watkins Landing to Huguenot Flatwater 177

29 Huguenot Flatwater to Ancarrow's Landing . . . 181

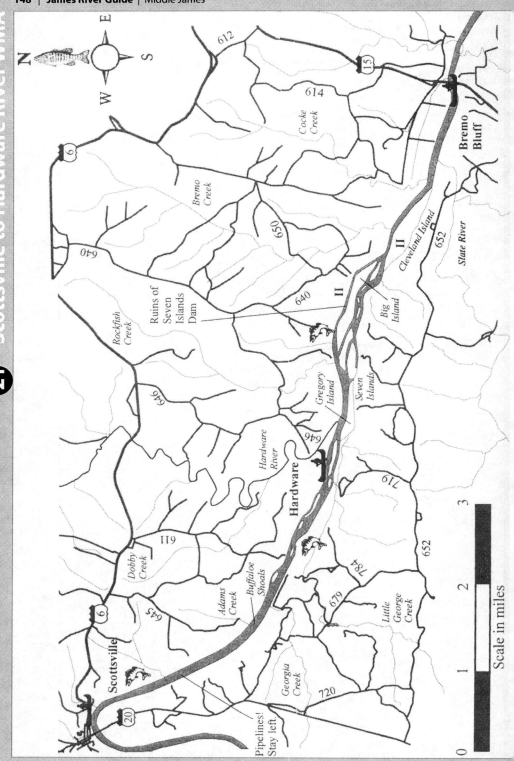

21 Scottsville to Hardware River WMA

TRIP: Scottsville to Hardware River Wildlife Management Area (WMA) in Buckingham and Fluvanna counties

USGS QUADS: Scottsville, Diana Mills, and Arvonia

DISTANCE: Six miles

MAP: Opposite, page 148

RAPIDS: None—numerous riffles

ACCESS: The put-in is on river left, located just downstream from the Route 20 Bridge and just off Route 6. The take-out is on river left, off Route 646. Be sure to hug the north bank (river left) as you near the take-out, or you may miss it. A number of islands dot the end of this section, and they can create confusion as to where to debark from the river. Both ramps are concrete and parking is available.

Since there are no rapids, the Scottsville float is ideal for novice paddlers. Canoeists of all levels can navigate this section in three hours or so. Fishermen will need no more than six hours to hit the best spots. Bird watchers and photographers will delight in the last two miles of the float as wooded shore-lines and islands harbor wildlife and offer fetching vistas.

I have tried to weave general fishing information into this narrative and here is another tidbit. Many anglers disdain hiring a guide to show them an unfamiliar section of a river, but I have always found that going with a local expert or guide on my initial trip makes good sense. A knowledgeable local angler or canoeist can point out potential danger spots, relate his past experiences on the water, detail the best fishing places, and explain where to observe wildlife, scoot through rapids, and take pictures.

I also always bring along *The James River Batteau Festival Trail guide* on any trip down the upper or middle sections. And when my experienced boatmate makes comments about a particular section, I jot down his comments on the publication. After that first trip, I usually feel competent enough not to need further assistance, especially on floats as free of potential danger as the Scottsville section. Of course, on rapid-filled sections, such as the Glasgow to Snowden trip on the headwaters or the Richmond white-water section, I always go with an expert paddler.

A hodgepodge of habitat greets the float fisherman on the first few miles of this section. About half a mile below Scottsville, the first fish-holding ground appears—several small islands with water willow and rocky cover. Riffles form around this habitat, and some considerable dropoffs exist immediately downstream.

One year on an October trip, I received no strikes on the initial pass through this area. Late October is often a difficult time to catch fish on the James. Smallmouths do not feed on the surface as often as they do in the late spring, summer, and early autumn, but they also have not permanently settled into their deep water fall and winter locales. Compounding the difficulty, the trees have shed some of their foliage, and leaves frequently foul surface flies and lures. So when I decided to pass through the section a second time, I opted for a Texas-rigged floating worm fished off the bottom. The seeming contradiction of a floating crawler, worked along the bottom, is not so bizarre after all. Floating worms consist of quite buoyant plastic, and they naturally rise off the substrate. Smallmouths often cling to the bottom at this season and anything shimmering along at eye level is very enticing to them. The Texas rig, which is a weedless one where the hook is burrowed into the body of the bait, results in very few snags. On that second pass, I received three strikes on the floating worm and landed a fine 15-inch bronzeback. This anecdote suggests that promising water should always be checked out several times before leaving it.

One mile into the Scottsville journey comes another smallmouth sanctuary, a deep rock-laden pool in the middle of the river. Many river anglers, just like their lake counterparts, often spend an entire trip cruising the shoreline, never exploring mid-river habitat. The easiest thing to do is drift aimlessly along the shoreline throughout a trip. Many, many James River banks are lined with rocks, logs, and depressions, and obviously are excellent places to fish. Many others, however, offer nothing more than shallow, sandy habitat. When you explore a section for the first time, periodically paddle to the mid-river areas. Often you will find some sensational cover. What's more, the fish here receive much less pressure than their bank-holding brethren.

Some one and one-half miles into the float, a pipeline crosses the river and creates some riffles. The river right bank provides the best passage, but even novices should experience no difficulty here. Spend some time casting to the aerated water below the pipeline. The next three miles offer little for the angler or canoeist. After you pass the pipeline, quickly paddle through half a mile of shallow water with little cover. The river deepens somewhat in the Buffalo Shoals area, but this locale offers only a few riffles and a slightly under-cut bank on river right. Make a few casts and continue downstream. The next mile or so constitutes an area known as "The Shallows." During bateau times, the many small boulders, combined with very shallow water, frequently re-sulted in the boats running aground. Areas like this draw smallmouths in the spring, but the heat of summer and the low water of fall make "The Shallows" unappealing to gamefish much of the year.

The last one and one-half miles of this float provides great pleasure for outdoors enthusiasts. Numerous small islands speckle the river, and the fish-ing, canoeing, photography, and wildlife watching are all terrific. Toss Woolly Buggers and jig-and-pigs to submerged rocks and logs that extend out from the islets. These two offerings are extremely reliable for autumn and throughout the year. What's more, the further along fall progresses, the more productive this duo becomes. Some individuals tip their jigs with real pork (the "pig" part of the lure), but I prefer one of the many soft plastic "pigs" now on the market. These trailers are much less messy to deal with than the real thing, which is packaged in a briny liquid. Plastic also does not dry out and become worthless as pork does after it has become exposed to the air for a while. The Woolly Bugger is a legendary big smallmouth pattern. One friend will employ nothing but a black Bugger on autumn float trips.

Canoeists will delight in exploring the many riffles that run along these islands. Since no serious rapids exist, paddlers can easily make their way upstream to check out interesting passageways between the islets. Many of these islands are fine places to take a break for a snack. I also like to beach the boat and take pictures. One of the most effective compositions along these islands is to situate the canoe at an angle to the shore, then wade up or downstream far enough that your field of view contains the boat, your companion, island, river, and sky. I often ask boatmates to wear bright colors such as blue, orange, yellow, and especially red. Even on drab looking days, red can add zest to a picture.

Wildlife watchers should be able to observe a number of species of water-fowl along the islands. Expect mallards and wood ducks to seek out the eddies. Canada geese, which were uncommon along the James in decades past, are now widespread along the stream. The fall period especially will bring a number of migratory ducks through this area.

On river left, the Hardware River Public Boat Landing indicates the conclusion of the Scottsville float. As mentioned in The Essentials section, be sure to hug the left shore-line toward the end of this trip. Occasionally, boaters have missed the ramp; an indication that you have done so will be if you come to the entrance of the Hardware River, a short distance below the ramp. Fortunately, the river flows quite mildly through here, and you will be able to paddle back upstream.

22 Hardware River WMA to Bremo Bluff

TRIP: Hardware River Wildlife Management Area (WMA) to Bremo Bluff (area also known as New Canton) in Buckingham and Fluvanna counties

USGS QUAD: Arvonia

DISTANCE: Seven miles

MAP: Page 154

RAPIDS: Several Class II rapids, numerous Class I rapids, and riffles

ACCESS: The put-in is on river left, off Route 646 which is itself off Route 6, just above where the Hardware River enters on the left. (Route 6 runs near the river for the rest of the coverage area of this book, making it a good highway with which to be familiar.) The take-out is on river right, just below the Route 15 Bridge. Both ramps are concrete, and parking is available.

The Hardware River float is my favorite on the middle river. The fishing is marvelous, the scenery is gorgeous, and the river's pace is brisk for the most part. Anglers will want to allot a good eight hours to fish this section while canoeists can cruise through in three to four hours. I would suggest that paddlers assign more time to the Hardware River WMA float, however, because it is such a fun one to explore.

The first mile of this jaunt lacks character, and I recommend that you quickly paddle through it, but the next three miles are a delight. The first major feature is the well-known Seven Islands area. The James River Batteau Festival Trail guide states that before sluices were constructed, this area was "one of the most dangerous places on the river." Now it is certainly one of the most alluring, as it features heavily wooded shorelines, numerous riffles and rapids, and lots of wildlife, especially waterfowl. And because of those sluices, or the passage of time, the former danger for the most part no longer exists.

Perhaps the best route through Seven Islands is along the river left bank. Actually, the term "Seven Islands" seems a bit of a misnomer because this section contains more than seven islets and islands. Many of the islands feature riffles or easy Class I rapids above and/or below them, and I have caught fine bass from these places. A good way to fish this area is to target the slick (calm water) just above a rapid and the first eddy below it. For example, on one trip

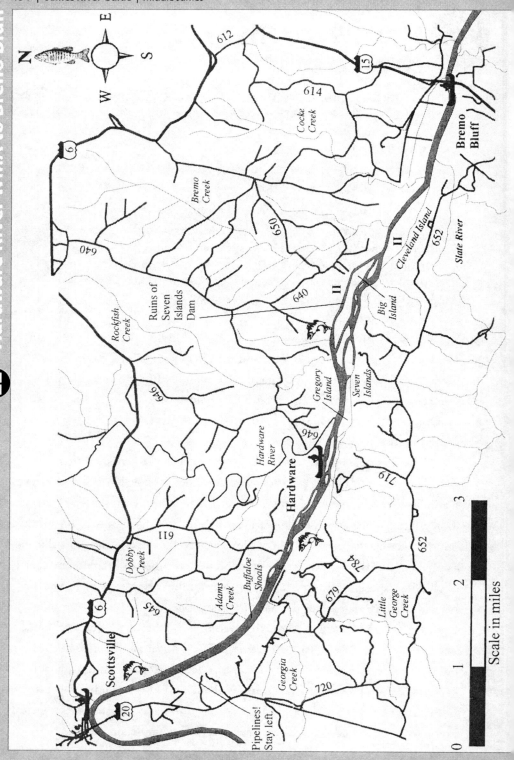

I caught a nice smallmouth that was feeding in the slick right before a rapid. The fish mauled a Phillips Crippled Killer that was twitched across the surface. On many occasions, I have a found a Sneaky Pete Popper to be similarly productive in this type of habitat.

In an eddy below another rapid, I drifted a four-inch ringworm past several submerged boulders and another large bass was the result. Ringworms are one of the premier soft plastic baits for river fishing. Their size and movement somewhat duplicates that of a hellgrammite, one of the favorite menu items of river smallmouths. As I wrote earlier, I don't believe that the color of a bait matters that much; most river runners, however, disagree with me on that topic and rely on black or brown soft plastics. Ringworms, because of the numerous ribs that constitute their bodies, also are great receptacles for fish scent which can sometimes attract indifferent bass. Fly-fishermen will want to try Murray's Black Marauders or Murray's Hellgrammites. The beauty of these two patterns,

Hardware River to Bremo Bluff is the premier float on the Middle James.

especially the latter, is that they can be presented up or downstream, or even cross current, and be readily attacked.

Part way through the Seven Islands area, you will spot the beginning of Big Island, aptly named because it extends for some two miles. This land form is so large that it is easy to mistake for the river left shoreline. The best route is to the right of the island, and again you will maneuver through numerous islets. On one trip in late spring, a friend and I observed a number of young wood ducks and mallards in this vicinity. Each flock was led by a female which quickly marshaled her young and departed as we neared. On several occasions, we stopped at the islands to take pictures. Written in the sand were the tell-tale footprints of the species that often visit these sanctuaries to forage; raccoon and great blue heron footprints were especially common, as were the shucked mussel shells that raccoons so love to crack. The discarded pincers and reamed-out shells of crawfish were other clues that a ringtail or two had recently dined well.

A Class II rapid heralds the end of the Big Island area. This is not a tricky Class II by any means; I like to split the middle of the rapid and other passages exist as well. Although I prefer the right route around Big Island because of the easy paddling and fine fishing, paddlers may want to consider the left circuit. This is a more confined and difficult passageway, but it offers several features of a historical nature. The ruins of Seven Islands Dam litter the left shore about a mile into the passage, and two sluices carved into the river are below the dam remains. Another sluice appears before the left passage reunites with the main river. Again, I must emphasize this route is much more confined than the right one, and novice or intermediate canoeists should probably avoid it. In the high water of late winter and early spring, the Class I and II rapids around both Seven Islands and Big Island often metamorphose into Class III rapids, making this float a better choice for low water conditions or the warm weather period.

The rest of this trip is not nearly as enticing, but is still pleasant enough. Cleveland Island looms toward river right about a half mile below the end of Big Island. The best passage by far is to the left. The left shore is liberally endowed with sycamores and silver maples, and it is possible to take a fish or two from the fallen trees along the bank. After Cleveland Island, the flow of the James slows noticeably and the main river becomes rather flat and featureless. At the five-mile mark of the trip, the Slate River—a fair smallmouth stream in its own right—enters on river right. Just before the Hardware River WMA float concludes, paddlers will have to deal with a final Class II rapid, Phelp's Falls. I recommend the "wave train" to the right of center. Wave trains, or standing waves, often intimidate novice boaters, but they usually offer safe passage. The downside of a standing wave is that it often douses the individual in the bow of a canoe, as I learned on this trip and on numerous others over the years. But unless your boat turns sideways midway through, a standing wave rarely causes serious difficulty. The Route 15 Bridge announces the end of this trip; the take-out is immediately downstream on river right.

Bremo Bluff to Coloumbia

23

Old Columbia Rd.

Columbia

Amphill Rd.

Micah Falls

Cobb's Island

069

Cobb Creek

069

686

690

White Rd.

Spicer's Island

654

Creek

659

Bouwright's Island

South

Chillisses Falls

Stearnes

019

734

15

6

652

655

655

Cole Creek

656

612

Holman Creek

15

670

614

Bear Garden Creek

672

670

Phelps Falls - II

US15

Cocke Creek

Bremo Bluff

15

N
W · E
S

Scale in miles

0   1   2   3

23 Bremo Bluff to Columbia

TRIP: Bremo Bluff (area also known as New Canton) to Columbia in Buckingham, Fluvanna, and Cumberland counties

USGS QUADS: Arvonia and Lakeside Village

DISTANCE: Eleven miles

MAP: Opposite, page 158

RAPIDS: Several Class I rapids and numerous riffles

ACCESS: The put-in is on river right at a concrete ramp, just below the Route 15 Bridge. Parking is available. The take-out is on river right just above the Route 690 Bridge at a concrete ramp. Parking is available.

Although the Bremo Bluff float is rather long, fishermen can easily spot the best lies, as well as the obvious places to skip. Anglers will need no more than six or seven hours tops to float this section. Canoeists can easily negotiate it in three to five hours.

At its inception, the Bremo Bluff float has little to recommend it for outdoor lovers. Within the first four miles, the major features are Cannon's Shoals (an uninteresting riffle less than a mile into the trip), a power plant (just downstream on river left), and straight, ordinary banks on both shores (for over two miles past the power plant). This is an uninspiring section, and I recommend you paddle through it quickly.

A little over four miles into the float, an outside bend appears on river right. Here, as on the middle river in general, the outside turns become increasingly less defined, becoming less round, shallower, and less likely to contain fish-attracting cover. For example, the bends on the headwaters and upper sections of the James are like a horseshoe and contain much wood debris. On the middle section, the curves are more like a horseshoe that has been partially straightened. And the further the river progresses toward Richmond, the less likely you are to encounter bends at all. The bend at this juncture provides some fair fishing for smallmouths and redbreast sunfish, but does not contain enough submerged wood cover to qualify it as a hot spot.

Well over a mile after this bend terminates, Chillisses' Falls appears. This riffle endures for several hundred yards. It is too shallow to offer much in the way of paddling excitement, but you should get in some fairly good fishing, particularly in the morning and evening. On my first Bremo Bluff float, I passed through Chillisses' Falls late in the evening and received numerous strikes from smallies that hit topwater baits. Chillisses' Falls also serves to indicate that the best fishing for the float is less than a mile downstream.

At the six-mile-point of this float, first Spicer's Island and then Boatwright's Island come into view. The area encompassed by these two islands offers some of the most attractive fish and wildlife habitat on the middle James. Spicer's features a number of cuts in its shoreline and within those cuts are water willow beds and underwater rocks. Islands that feature smooth, round sides are much less likely to attract good numbers of fish. But islands such as Spicer's that have suffered the ravages of erosion and current over the decades are true fish magnets.

Immediately downstream, Boatwright's Island flaunts just as many indentations and fish cover as Spicer's. In fact, the James has literally carved up this island, and bits and pieces of it are separated by eddies and riffles. On my initial Bremo Bluff float, my companion was outfitter John Garman of

Working the edges between Bremo Bluff and Columbia.

Fredericksburg. We selected an islet to pitch a tent for the evening. There is something special about spending a summer night along the James. I love to identify birds by their songs, and dozens of species rear their young on this river. Garman is a novice birder. While he cooked dinner I regaled him with tales of how to distinguish one species' song from that of another. I feel it is much easier to figure out what kind of bird is singing if you can turn the songster's notes into human words or phrases. For example, one of the birds that nests on Boatwright's is the acadian flycatcher. I believe what the acadian "says" is "flea-check, flea-check." Other birders claim that this flycatcher shouts out "piz-za, piz-za." Whether the acadian flycatcher clamors for airborne insects or a fast food entree is up to you, but using "bird phonics" is a fun and effective way to learn songs.

Other birds that we heard singing included pee-wees, blue-gray gnatcatchers, and orchard orioles. After the birds of the day ceased their songs, the birds of the evening took over. A whip-poor-will began its lilting complaint just as a full moon appeared in the night sky and later a great horned owl began to boom out in the distance. Then a thunderstorm quickly appeared on the horizon, flirted with the island for a few minutes, and finally hurried on downstream, leaving just the sound of the river to send us off to sleep. If you love the James River, you owe it to yourself to spend at least one night on its shores.

The next morning Garman and I were on the river at sunrise, but we experienced poor sport even though there are numerous places to fish along Boatwright's. I had predicted the evening before that such would be the case because of the full moon. I can not say scientifically why "full moon mornings" offer such wretched fishing, but from my many years as a river fisherman and from talking to a number of veteran river rats, many of us have noticed the same thing. The prevalent theory is that on the night of a full moon, the fish feed heavily and then rest throughout most of the next morning. The after-noon after a full moon typically ushers in some outstanding sport. In short, there is little reason to be on the water early when the moon waxes full.

A half mile below Boatwright's, check out the right shoreline for a goodly amount of rock and wood cover. At the 8.5 mile point of the Bremo Bluff float, Cobb's Island comes into view. Paddlers should select the river right passage because it holds more water and some riffles that send you briskly downstream. The left side is probably better for fishermen, however, because it hosts a number of laydowns on the river left shoreline. These are good places to cast topwater baits early and late in the day.

Cobb's Falls, an easy Class I, comes at the end of the island on its right side and offers some fishing opportunities. Plenty of large rocks give character to the pool below this rapid. Micah Falls lies just downstream, but this is "skinny water"—that is, shallow water with a pebble bottom—and is not worth casting to. A rock ledge appears at the ten-mile juncture of the float and is really the last place where anglers can expect to catch many fish. The Columbia landing is next on the agenda, on river right just above the Route 690 Bridge.

24 Columbia to Cartersville

TRIP: Columbia to Cartersville in Cumberland, Fluvanna, and Goochland counties

USGS QUADS: Lakeside Village and Cartersville

DISTANCE: Nine and one-half miles

MAPS: Page 164

RAPIDS: A few riffles

ACCESS: The put-in is on river right just above the Route 690 Bridge. The ramp is concrete and parking is available. The take-out is just below the Route 45 Bridge on river right. The ramp is concrete and parking is available.

This book covers numerous float trips that outdoor enthusiasts can take on the James, and of all these outings, I would rate the Columbia excursion as the least appealing for smallmouth bass anglers. Fish-holding cover is scarce, rapids are lacking, and outside bends are virtually nonexistent. That said, you might read one year where the state record smallmouth was caught from this float—and I guess such an occurrence is possible. But, all and all, smallmouth fishermen would be better served to go elsewhere. Canoeists who enjoy white water should also avoid this float; there is simply no white water to pump the adrenaline.

So just who would enjoy the Columbia float? Canoeists who have never floated a river would relish this trip as a "get acquainted with rivers" voyage. Paddle time is five to six hours even for the most inexperienced. Parents wishing to introduce children to fishing would find this trip inviting because redbreast sunfish seem to inhabit almost every submerged stick and undercut bank on the Columbia trek. Although redbreasts are not large—typically running five to eight inches—they bite willingly and offer something that many youngsters crave: continuous action and fun. Twelve-inch and smaller smallmouths also flourish in this section, and they, too, can provide sport for budding anglers.

Abundant bird life is another reason to undergo this trip. On one Columbia float, I glimpsed a bald eagle, and I also watched an immature red-tail hawk harass two young wood ducks. The woodies were in no danger from the hawk, which had yet to learn that its talons and flight skills were not equipped for plucking ducks from a stream. My boatmate and I also observed a hen turkey shepherding her young along a wooded shoreline, and we spied an osprey flying overhead. Even on the most uninteresting stretches of the James, you

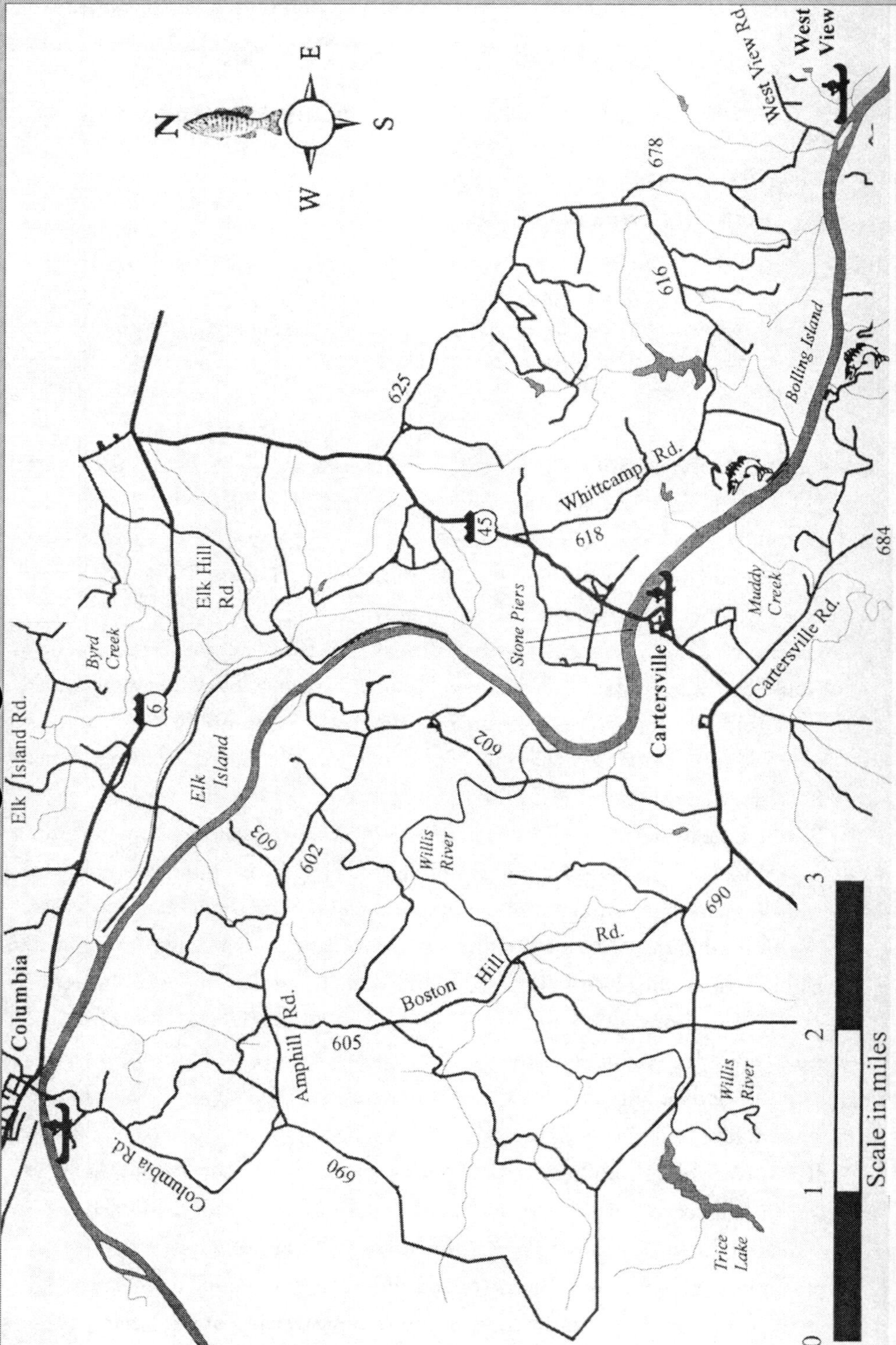

West View Rd.

West View

678

616

Bolling Island

684

625

45

Whittcamp Rd.

618

Muddy Creek

Stone Piers

Cartersville Rd.

Cartersville

Elk Hill Rd.

Byrd Creek

6

Elk Island Rd.

Elk Island

602

603

602

Willis River

Rd.

690

Columbia

Amphill Rd.

Boston Hill

605

Columbia Rd.

069

Willis River

Trice Lake

0 1 2 3

Scale in miles

should enjoy quality wildlife watching. But, again, if jumbo bass and roaring rapids are your interests, go elsewhere.

My initial Columbia trip took place during the annual eight-day James River Batteau Festival in mid-June, and I enjoyed observing these craft powered by individuals in authentic nineteenth-century garb. Bateaux ran forty to sixty feet long and featured wide walkways used by boatmen as they poled up or down the river. Introduced in the 1700s, bateaux carried hogsheads of tobacco and other goods to Richmond. In 1784, George Washington came before the Virginia General Assembly with a plan to improve navigation on the James and from that speech, the James River Company came into existence, with Washington as its first president. The objective of the company was to spread commerce westward as part of America's manifest destiny. Toward that end, workers—often slaves and impoverished immigrants—cut canals, built locks, and improved navigation. These workers often complained bitterly of the extremely arduous work, and a commission or two was appointed to study their plight. But canal labor continued to be a back-breaking and dangerous affair.

Over the ensuing decades, those who followed Washington as movers and shakers of the James River Company cannot be said to have lacked imagination and drive. In 1812, Chief Justice John Marshall led a commission that proclaimed the James could be linked with the Ohio River by means of a canal and a wagon road from Buchanan to the Great Falls of the Kanawha in modern day West Virginia. By 1835, the project had become known as the James River and Kanawha Company, and many people today who point to the ruins of the scheme along the river refer to them as the "Kanawha Canal stones." By the early 1840s, packet boats were using the canal. I asked Scottsville's John Bowers, an amateur historian, about the origin of the term "packet" boat. John said that a possible explanation was that people and cargo were quite "packed" or cramped in the boats and that these craft took some 40 hours to travel from Lynchburg to Richmond, a distance of 147 miles. By the early 1850s, the canal had been completed to Buchanan, a distance of 197 miles. Of that mileage, 160 miles consisted of canals and 37 miles existed as slack water on the river.

The James River and Kanawha Canal survived for 45 years; two events served to kill it. In March 1865, General Sheridan entered Scottsville and proceeded to wreck the canal for miles upstream and down from the town. That event was disastrous enough, but the real culprit for the canal's demise was the increasing importance and presence of the railroads. Interestingly, the college of Washington and Lee in Lexington to this day receives $3,000 annually as part of the interest on stock that George Washington owned in the old James River Company. And the canal continues to contribute fish habitat and historical charm to the river. The lesson of history is that no mode of transportation is permanent, whether it is a bateau, packetboat, railroad, or the modern-day automobile.

John Bowers recommends that those who want to read more about the bateau and canal era read *Waterway to the West* by James J. Kirkwood, published by the Eastern National Parks and Monument Association. Much of what he knows about this part of Virginia history, says John, comes from this small booklet.

The major landmarks of this float can be quickly summarized. Elk Island looms at the one-mile point and continues for approximately half the trip. The right channel is your only option. Some concrete piers, all that are left from a bridge, indicate that you are about two and one-half miles from the put-in, and a riffle area comes into view just before the four-mile point. Here and there, some downed trees along the banks will serve as sanctuaries for small bass and hordes of redbreast sunfish. In fact, on one trip, a number of sunnies battered a one-fourth ounce buzzbait—an extremely aggressive act for a fish this small. Between seven and eight miles into the float, the Willis River enters on river right, and ten more minutes of paddling brings you to the take-out below the Route 45 Bridge on river right. Directly above that structure are some stone piers of an earlier bridge.

25 Cartersville to West View

TRIP: Cartersville to West View in Cumberland, Goochland, and Powhatan counties

USGS QUAD: Cartersville

DISTANCE: Five miles

MAP: page 164

RAPIDS: A few small riffles

ACCESS: The put-in is just below the Route 45 Bridge on river right. The take-out is on river left, just to the left of a small island. Route 643 leads to the take-out. Both access points have concrete ramps and parking is available.

The Cartersville float is well-suited for an afternoon of fishing, while canoeists can easily scoot through it in a few hours. This trip offers only fair fishing for smallmouth bass, but anglers after redbreast sunfish will find that this excursion to be a regular mecca. The omnipresent panfish is small, but bites willingly. Fly-fishermen can have a ball casting small poppers and spider and beetle imitations. White water enthusiasts will find this trip wanting. The steep, wooded hillsides provide some nice scenery, but the flat water and the lack of islets and shoals, so characteristic of much of the middle river, leave this excursion lacking in flavor. However, novice canoeists may want to undergo this easy five-miler if they have yet to find their "sea legs" on the James.

I initially floated this section as part of a 45-mile odyssey down the James with John Garman of Fredericksburg. One of the great aspects of spending several days on any stream with someone is that you can learn new tactics about fishing, canoeing, and, in this case, how to plan for a multiple-day trip. On the previous overnights that my wife Elaine and I had taken, we packed essentials such as sleeping bags and a tent, but all the accessories such as water bottles, tins of food, and cooking utensils tended to overburden our craft. Garman is an expert at simplifying the load.

Garman toted the usual items such as a tent and two sleeping bags with accompanying pads, but his other gear reflected a pleasing minimalist philosophy. For example, he brought no water at all. He instead employs a Mountain Safety Research (MSR) Waterworks Filter that filters out all bacteria, including giardia. Giardia causes an infamous affliction known colloquially as "beaver fever," causing intense bouts of intestinal distress. Garman placed the tube from the filter into the river and in a few minutes we had cool, clear water that is purported to be 99.999 percent safe to drink. Garman says the number one mistake canoe campers make is bringing numerous jugs of water, making paddling more arduous and the canoe unbalanced. A water filter eliminates these problems.

John Garman transforms the James into potable water.

Another common error, Garman pointed out, is conveying a heavy cook stove or grill downstream. Instead, Garman relies on an MSR stove that burns on propane and can be ready to cook on in two minutes. On our first night, he employed an MSR stove and a two-quart pot to concoct a scrumptious dinner of chicken and rice with broccoli. The rice furnishes much-needed carbohydrates for fast energy, and the cheese supplies fat for slow release energy all day. This entree came in a lightweight freeze-dried pouch, and the water, of course came from the James, courtesy of the filter. Garman "set the table" with a few plastic cups, eating utensils, and plates, which can be washed with the purified water and used for the next meal. Garman employed the stove in the mornings as well. The device cooked oatmeal, grits, and coffee, all of which can be stored in lightweight bags. Garman prefers peanut butter and honey sandwiches for lunch, which provide plenty of energy and do not require a stove.

All this equipment, plus a change of clothes and toiletries, fits neatly into two dry bags the size of a large suitcase. We stored the bags in the middle of the canoe for balance. The water purifier was left out, so that Garman could pump water at any point on our float. At night, this thoroughly organized outfitter could set up camp and be cooking dinner in less than a half hour. In the past, Elaine and I often took more than an hour to do the same, with much less desirable results.

Garman also passed on three more small tips that I had never considered. I had always looked for sand beaches to set up tents, but Garman prefers pebble beaches because they do not hold moisture like sand. Sand is also highly abrasive and very hard on camping gear. Garman's second tip involves setting up a tent on what the guide calls the "non-leeward" side of an island. That is, he prefers the side of an island that receives the full brunt of the prevailing breezes so that insects will have a more difficult time zeroing in on the campsite. Finally, he suggests that canoe campers never build a fire. Although a campfire may be aesthetically pleasing to those around it, the next sojourners at that locale may not find the fire rings appealing, especially if a number of such human reminders pockmark the area. When Garman and I broke camp, there were no reminders of our visit. Since canoeists on the James and other rivers will sometimes have to depend on gaining permission from landowners to camp, this is an important consideration for all of us who want to continue to enjoy the waterway.

The Cartersville trip itself can be easily summarized. The first two miles consist of shallow water with a mostly pebble bottom, and I suggest that you quickly paddle through it. On river left, a heavily-wooded shoreline then commences, offering some fair wood cover. I have dueled with bass along this bank, and numerous sunfish lurk to attack any fly or lure that is tossed. This shoreline continues for approximately two miles. After that you'll encounter some small riffles and rock pools that provide the best fishing on the Cartersville float. But even this locale does not compare favorably to the excellent midstream habitat so common on other sections of the river.

The take-out is to the left side of an island and is easily spotted from several hundred yards upstream.

26

West View to Maidens

N
E
S
W

Fairground Road

Maidens Road

State Farm

Beaverdam Creek

Lee Rd. 628

Pleasant's Island

Huguendt Tr.

Old River Tr.

Maidens

6

522

6

Cedar Point

617

Little Creek

Little Creek Culvert

Old River Tr.

522

Mohawk Creek

Jefferson
618

Landing Rd.

Cosby Rd.

621

522

Maidens Adventure Dam (stay left of center)

Lock
Canal
Lock
Cut stone remains of dam

Lickinghole Creek

Rock Castle Rd.

600

Red Rock Shoals

627

Ben Lomond Rd.

Rock Castle

Three Bridges Road

West View Rd. 643

Mosby Island

Deep Creek

Rock Castle Falls (stay to center)

Bell Rd.

684

Cartersville Rd.

West View

Scale in miles

0   1   2   3

TRIP: West View to Maidens in Powhatan and Goochland counties
USGS QUADS: Cartersville and Goochland
DISTANCE: Eleven and one-half miles
MAP: Opposite, page 170
RAPIDS: A number of easy Class I rapids and many small riffles
ACCESS: The concrete ramp put-in is on river left, just to the left of a small island. Route 643 leads to the access point. Parking is available. The river right concrete ramp take-out is immediately above the Route 522 Bridge. Parking is available.

The West View section of the James is one of the better trips on the middle river. Anglers should plan to spend about eight hours here, and paddlers will find five to six hours sufficient. Portions of this outing are quite photogenic, especially the Class I rapids, riffles, and islets that appear in the first half of the float.

One of those photo opportunities occurs at the put-in. Shutterbugs may want to paddle downstream a few yards from the access point and take a shot of the island that cleaves the river. The best route is to the right of the island, and anglers will find a good many dropoffs and some wood cover. A mile into this journey comes a several-hundred-yard section replete with shoals, humps, and deep water. A good approach for working midriver cover is to identify individual dropoffs and rocks that hold fish, and then record in a notebook the location of these honey holes. An angler can do this by lining up features (such as trees, boulders, and buildings) along both shorelines with these hot spots or by employing the Global Positioning System (GPS). More and more river and lake fishermen are using GPS to orient themselves and to relocate offshore cover. Try Wooly Buggers, Muddler Minnows, jig-and-pigs, and plastic lizards and ringworms to entice these smallmouths.

Near the two-mile juncture of the West View trek looms the Rock Castle Falls area, sporting some capital bass habitat. Scads of riffles, easy Class I rapids, and islets of water willow constitute this locale. Dropoffs, underwater rocks, and some shaded banks add character as well, making this a place anglers will want to linger.

On the West View float I took with outfitter John Garman, we watched the sky darken as a thunderstorm appeared imminent. Only once while on a river have a companion and I been caught in a violent storm—on that occasion we experienced lightning strikes within a hundred yards of us. Garman says he takes a number of steps both before and during a trip to avoid being caught in a similar situation.

"Some good preliminary steps are to check the Weather Channel forecast before your trip and to contact a canoe livery about current weather conditions," he says. "You should also learn about current water levels and conditions on the river. For instance, a river that is already running high can't stand the extra water that a storm may bring, whereas a low, clear stream may be able to withstand a heavy thunderstorm and not rise too much. Once you're on a stream and a surprise storm appears to be brewing, I recommend that you check the 'depth of the storm.' That is, does the storm cover the entire sky, and can you see to the back of it? If the storm blankets the sky, it is best to get off the river immediately. If it is 'patchy' and if it does not appear to be heading toward you, usually there is not too much to worry about."

Classic smallmouths habitat returns to the James on the West View to Maidens float.

Garman says he also likes to ascertain the speed of a tempest. If the weather pattern is scudding rapidly toward you, the wind is increasing, and air temperature is decreasing, you could be in for quite a downpour accompanied by thunder and lightning. If such a storm is about to occur in mid-afternoon, which is typical on the James, then the outfitter says he makes camp for the evening. To guard against the rising river, Garman looks for a site that is at least ten feet above the river, hauling the canoe up with him. Many people will show enough common sense to camp well away from the river, only to find that their canoe has been swept away during the night.

I usually don't put too much stock in folklore, but there is one case when I do. When growing up, I heard that birds and frogs often heralded a storm. As I grew older and learned how to identify the songs of wildlife, I learned that the "coo-coo-coo" of the yellow-billed cuckoo and the trill of the gray tree frog often meant that a storm is imminent, especially as the clouds begin to darken. Listen for these two creatures while on a river and be forewarned.

Deep Creek enters on river right below Rock Castle Falls and signals the end of this area. At the two and one-half mile marker, a series of easy Class I rapids and riffles begin and continue for approximately a mile. This is yet another fine place to wet a line, for many of these swift water locales offer exemplary fishing above and below them. You'll find some good rock habitat as well, especially in the vicinity of the first Class I or riffle. The actual force of the rapid depends upon water levels. During the warm water period, topwaters of all kinds will produce in this section, and canoeists will find these rapids refreshing to scoot through.

At the four-mile point, a weak outside bend occurs on river right and fair bank cover speckles the shoreline for a hundred or so yards. The next four miles, however, provide little in angling potential. The only highly visible marker is at mile eight where the Lickinghole Creek Aqueduct resides, above where the creek of the same name enters the James on river left. At the nine-mile point, some downed trees create smallmouth and sunfish sanctuaries at a weak outside bend on river left. The remaining two and one-half miles of the West View trip feature some quality midstream holding areas, but anglers have to search the river diligently to find these areas and may wish to record them in a notebook. If you are willing to do this extra bit of work, you can catch fish which rarely have a lure or fly presented properly to them. The Route 522 Bridge concludes the West Fork float.

27

676
621
623
621
Watkin's
Landing
612
621
652
676
6
Little River
Sabot Island
644
711
Little River
Sabot Island
654
641
642
614
Genito Creek
670
6
711
Jude's
Fish Dam
670
628
615
Pleasant's Island
632
645
State
Farm
Bridge
711
Remains of
Maiden's
Adventure
Dam
634
632
6
Hughes Creek
617
711
615
522
522
Michaux
Bridge
607
711
6
522
Powhatan
State Park

N
E
W
S

Scale in Miles

3

2

1

0

621

27 Maidens to Watkins Landing

TRIP: Maidens to Watkins Landing in Powhatan and Goochland counties

USGS QUADS: Goochland, Perkinsville, Fine Creek Mills, and Midlothian

DISTANCE: Thirteen miles

MAP: Opposite, page 174

RAPIDS: A number of easy Class I rapids and many small riffles

ACCESS: At Maidens, a concrete ramp exists on river right off U.S. Route 522. Parking is available in a gravel lot. At Watkins, a concrete ramp exists on river right off Route 652. Parking is available in a spacious lot.

The first two miles of the Maiden float feature slow, sandy shallow water, patches of elodea and other vegetation, Hughes Creek entering on river right, and scattered sub-surface boulders that create boils. The first area worth serious smallmouth fishing is just before the two-mile mark where the remains of Maiden's Adventure Dam create a Class I drop.

The next two miles offers the odd boulder field, star grass flats, the occasional rifle and the State Farm Bridge spanning the James. River smallmouth fans may want to know when the great fishing begins. Well, for the next seven miles, some of the best stream smallie habitat I have encountered anywhere in Virginia awaits.

Harry Byrd, IV with a nice smallmouth he caught on the Maidens trip.

At the four-mile point, you will see an island and then the superlative sport starts. For below this island, lies a series of small to medium size islands, plus water willow islets and the accompanying riffles. In the space of one hour through here with friends Harry Byrd, IV and Allan Lott, both of Richmond, we caught a number of quality-size smallmouths between 12 and 14 inches, all on crankbaits and spinnerbaits.

My smallies all came on a Cordell Big O crankbait. I try not to have favorite lures in any category of baits no matter whether they are soft plastics, blade baits, crankbaits, or whatever. But goodness gracious, the Big O has been a very good artificial for a very long time for me. The hard plastic bait runs about four-feet deep, just perfect for an upland river like the James, and the rapid back and forth movements of its wobble seem to draw brown bass. Whenever I am struggling to catch fish and I feel that a crankbait is the best choice to improve my fortunes, I often turn to the legendary Big O.

The James next makes a short river right bend and more islands and riffles characterize the curve. The river then straightens, Fine Creek enters on river right, more islets appear, followed by Pleasant's Island, which extends for about a mile or until about 7 ½ miles into the junket. Below Pleasant's Island, you'll encounter numerous riffles, boulders, boils, and bronzebacks. You'll also see Genito Creek enter on river left. All of these areas teem with smallmouths and are well worth spending time checking out.

Sabot Island looms at the nine-mile point; take the channel down the land mass' right shoreline. More great riverine cover exists in the form of ledges and boulders, as well as some quality bank cover in the form of box elders and sycamores. A series of small islands and riffles then characterize this section. A small rapid forms here, Manakin Falls, but it is nothing more than a Class I at best. At about the 12-mile point, the marvelous mossyback habitat ends, and you will have to paddle a mile or so to reach the river right Watkins Landing take-out.

For the trip as a whole, my advice is to fish sparingly the first four miles, budget your time so that you can spend a great deal of time among all the islands and islets (so many exist and the habitat is so outstanding that you can't possibly work everything—but try anyway) and then paddle non-stop the last mile of the float. What an excursion! This is not only one of the best trips on the Middle James but also on the river as a whole.

28 Watkins Landing to Huguenot Flatwater

TRIP: Watkins Landing to Huguenot Flatwater in Powhatan and Goochland counties

USGS QUADS: Midlothian and Bon Air

DISTANCE: Ten miles

MAP: Page 178

RAPIDS: A few riffles below Boshers dam

ACCESS: At Watkins, a concrete ramp exists on river right off Route 652. Parking is available in a spacious lot. At Huguenot Flatwater, a wood canoe slide exists on river right off Riverside Drive. Parking is available in a spacious lot.

If smallmouth bass are your favorite game fish, the Watkins Landing float is lacking in charms as basically it is a long trek through the backwaters of Boshers Dam. However, if you own a power boat and enjoy angling for largemouths and flathead catfish, then you will like this section. From Watkins Landing to Boshers Dam, you will have eight miles to fish. The river flows fairly straight throughout, and the major cover is downed, shoreline trees, sycamore root wads, curly leaf pondweed beds, and the odd water willow stand. Bernards Creek enters on river right about four miles below Watkins. I don't like the sameness of fishing this type of water, but, again, moving water smallies are my passion and if lake largemouths are your desire, then this water is for you.

If you should decide to make a through canoe trip, you can portage around Boshers Dam on river left. Below the dam to the take out, riffles, elodea beds, and a boulder and islet garden (near the end) characterize the final two miles of the Watkins getaway. This section is very much worth fishing for river smallies, but instead of paddling eight miles and undergoing a portage to reach it, just paddle upstream from the Huguenot access point. You could paddle up one side of the river, stopping frequently to explore likely areas, then drift back the other side to do the same.

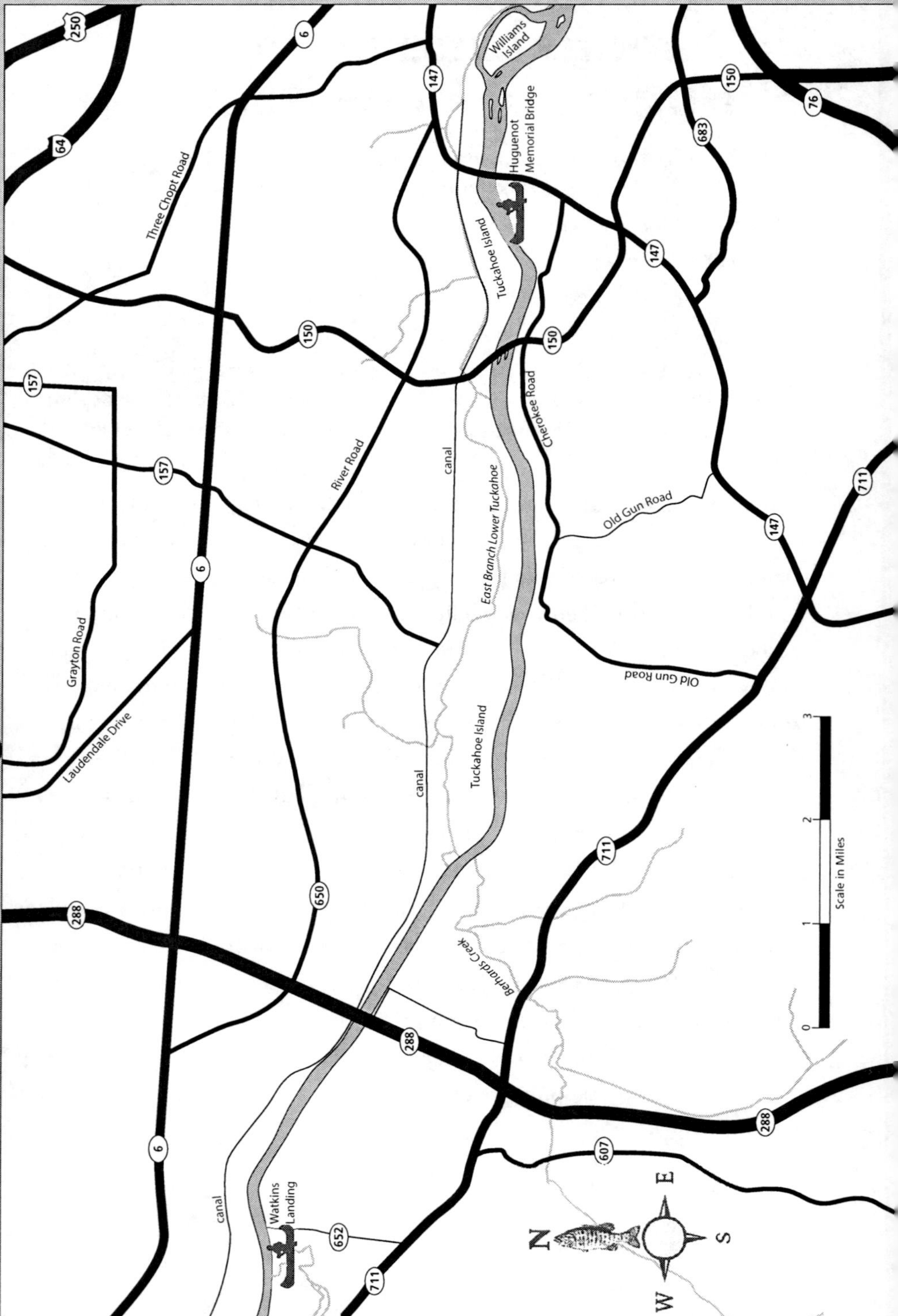
Williams Island
Huguenot Memorial Bridge
Tuckahoe Island
Three Chopt Road
River Road
canal
East Branch Lower Tuckahoe
Cherokee Road
Old Gun Road
Grayton Road
Laudendale Drive
Tuckahoe Island
Old Gun Road
Scale in Miles
0
1
2
3
Berhards Creek
Watkins Landing
N
E
S
W
250
64
6
147
150
76
683
157
711
650
288
607
652

The author's son Mark with a huge flathead caught in the Watkins area.

29 Huguenot Flatwater to Ancarrow's Landing

RICHMOND

Ancarrow's Landing

Commerce Road

Maury Street

Brook Road

Monument Avenue

Forest Hill Avenue

Williams Island

Riverside Drive

Cherokee Road

Huguenot Memorial Bridge

canal

Scale in Miles

29 Huguenot Flatwater to Ancarrow's Landing

TRIP: Huguenot Flatwater to Ancarrow's Landing in Richmond

USGS QUADS: Bon Air and Richmond

DISTANCE: Nine miles

MAPS: Opposite, page 180

RAPIDS: Class Is to Vs

ACCESS: At Huguenot Flatwater, a wood canoe slide exists on river right off Riverside Drive. Parking is available in a spacious lot. At Ancarrow's Landing, a concrete ramp exists on river right off Brander Street via Maury Street. Parking is available in a spacious lot.

In my opinion, the Huguenot Flatwater float flaunts the most intense, perilous, sustained whitewater in the Old Dominion. Although I took this trip for the first time in a canoe with Gray McDermid of Richmond, I will never again debark in such a craft on this section. Caution: do not take this getaway in a canoe unless you are an exceptional paddler. I recommend taking it as three other members of my party (Harry Byrd, Alan Lott, and Richard Lesko, all of Richmond) did—in a kayak or perhaps in a raft manned by a professional. Even then, you will have to frequently portage and be extremely vigilant, as this trip contains rapids that can, and have, caused people to lose their lives.

The first mile of the trip gives no inkling of what is to come. Scattered islets and riffles characterize this section, and this is a great area to work crankbaits, grubs, and streamers through the swiftly flowing water. Then you will come to Williams Island. Take the right channel so as to avoid a dam on the island's left side. However, the remains of Z Dam lie on the right side near the beginning of Williams. I have run this low water dam in a raft, but if you are in a canoe or kayak, I recommend portaging Z on its left side along the island. Byrd and Lesko maintain that this section receives heavy fishing pressure as Riverside Drive runs parallel to the James.

The Class II Pony Pasture rapid comes next followed by a boulder garden and riffles. You will have to bob and weave through Pony Pasture or portage it on river right. For the next three miles, you will drift through very shallow water characterized by riffles and scattered boulders until you arrive at the Powhite Ledges, which lie above and below the Powhite Bridge. At this point, you have basically entered the fall line where the James metamorphoses from a Piedmont to a Tidewater waterway and the river drops some 80 feet in three miles. And as students of topography know, fall lines typically mean, and in this case most certainly do, drastic drops in the stream bottom.

Next come a railroad bridge and a train themed rapid—Choo-Choo, a solid Class II. McDermid and I elected to avoid Choo-Choo by navigating a narrow channel on far river left. The standard way to avoid the rapid, though, is to go to its right. You are now about four miles below the Huguenot access point. Then come more Class I and II riffles and Boulevard Avenue Bridge. Below this structure, you will encounter many more rapids that can rate from Class I to III depending on water levels.

The smallmouth fishing through here is outstanding. The best approach is to portage a rapid, beach your boat on a water willow bed and fan cast the surrounding area. If you decide to wade, I strongly recommend that you wear a life jacket. Indeed, you should always wear your life jacket this entire trip. I never take my life jacket off on any river, but, again, and I cannot emphasize this too much, not wearing one can mean death on whitewater like that which exists here.

The next major feature is Hollywood Dam, followed by Belle Isle and its namesake rapids, and the U.S Route 1/301 Robert E. Lee Bridge. So many Class III and IV rapids exist through this section that my party made no attempt to run them. McDermid and I portaged over the dam's structure and then walked and dragged the craft through riffles and water willow beds so as to avoid the

The Huguenot Flatwater float features some intense rapids but also offers calmer sections where the fishing is good.

white-water. At one point, an hour elapsed for us to go just 100 yards or so. Again, this is a dangerous, potentially life threatening area. You are now about six miles below the put-in.

After a few hundred yards come to two more very dangerous structures: Brown's Island Dam remains and the Manchester Canal Dam. The U.S. 60 Bridge comes between them. In normal and moderate water levels, Class IV rapids exist and they can become Class V at high water events. Adding to the danger is the exposed rebar and jagged chunks and remains of the dams, not to mention hydraulics and boulders. This is big smallmouth water, so allot plenty of time here. Topwater baits such as Tiny Torpedos and Crippled Killers work well here. Brown's Island is probably best portaged on river left. I portaged Manchester on its right side. This chapter does not give you enough information to run these rapids. For that information, you would need a white water guide book.

After you pass Mayo Island and Mayo Bridge (which crosses the James above the island) and go under the I-95 Bridge, you will have to paddle over a mile to reach Ancarrow's Landing. There are still riffles in this section, but the pace of water is nothing like that which is upstream. Of all the river fishing trips I have ever taken, this one stressed and tired me the most. Instead of making a through trip as I did, a better and more productive approach to fishing this section should probably involve putting in and taking out at the access points that exist on this section. That way you can experience some quality fishing without having to portage, or goodness gracious, run these rapids. Alan Lott says that many anglers put in at the Huguenot Woods or Pony Pasture access points and take out at Reedy Creek. Below Reedy Creek is the domain of whitewater thrill seekers. Those access points are as follows.

Pony Pasture: Wood canoe slide located below Pony Pasture Rapid on river right off Riverside Drive and two miles below the Huguenot access point. Parking is available in a spacious lot.

Reedy Creek: No ramp, canoe/kayak access only on river right with about a 50-yard walk from a small parking lot. Access point is on Riverside Drive via 42nd Street and Forest Hill Avenue. The Reedy Creek access point is located four miles below the Pony Pasture one.

Thus ends this book's coverage of the upper reaches of the James. I hope this book will add to your enjoyment of a waterway sometimes called "America's River." It is my home river and by far, my favorite one to visit.

APPENDIX A: Trip Planner

The key to any successful trip down the James is careful planning. Following are sources of information, all of which I have used and can recommend.

General Information Sources

Allegheny Highlands Blueway
AlleghanyHighlandsBlueway.com

Float Fishermen of Virginia
FloatFishermen.org

James River Association
JamesRiverAssociation.org

National Weather Service
ERH.noaa.gov/marfc/james.shtml

Upper James River Water Trail
UpperJamesRiverWaterTrail.com

USGS Current Water Data for Virginia
WaterData.USGS.gov/va/nwis/rt

Land Protection: Conservation Easements

Blue Ridge Conservancy
BlueRidgeConservancy.org

Blue Ridge Land Conservancy
BlueRidgeLandConservancy.org

DCR Office of Land Conservation
DCR.virginia.gov/land_
conservation/index.shtml

Land Trust Alliance
LandTrustAlliance.org

New River Conservancy
NewRiverConservancy.org

New River Land Trust
NewRiverLandTrust.org

Valley Conservation Council
ValleyConservation.org

VDACS Office of Farmland Preservation VDACS.virginia.gov/
preservation

Virginia Department of Forestry
DOF.virginia.gov

Virginia Outdoors Foundation
VirginiaOutdoorsFoundation.org

Guides, Canoe Liveries, and Outfitters

Angler's Lane
Graves Mill Shopping Cener
Forest, VA 24551
434-385-0200
AnglersLane.com

Confluence Outfitters
434-941-9550
ConfluenceOutfittersVA.com

Dead Drift Flies
DeadDriftFlies.com

Discover the James
804-938-2350
DiscoverTheJames.com

H&H Outdoors
17518 Main Street
Buchanan, VA 24066
540-254-2420

James River Reeling & Rafting
265 Ferry Street
Scottsville, VA 24590
804-286-4FUN
ReelingAndRafting.com

James River Runners
10082 Hatton Ferry Road
Scottsville, VA 24590
434-286-2338
JamesRiver.com

Mossy Creek Fly Fishing
1790 E Market St #92
Harrisonburg, VA 22801
540-434-2444
MossyCreekFlyFishing.com

New Angle Fishing Company
540-354-1774
Facebook.com/
NewAngleFishingCompany/info

New River Outdoor Company
(parent company of James River
Outdoor Company and Southern
Muskie Guide Service)
540-921-7438
ICanoeTheNew.com
SouthernMuskieGuideService.com
NewRiverOutdoorcompany.com

Orvis
19 Campbell Ave., Roanoke, VA 24010
540-345-3635
Orvis.com/roanoke

Outdoor Trails
Botetourt Commons, 28 Kingston Dr.
Daleville, VA 24083
540-9925850

Riders Up Outfitters
540-862-7999
RidersUpOutfitters.com

RockonCharters
540-354-9424 or 588-6628
RockOnCharters.net

South River Fly Shop
317 West Main Street
Waynesboro, VA 22980
540-942-5566
SouthRiverFlyShop.com

Tracy Asbury
West Virginia Outdoor Adventures
1-888-PLAYWVA

Twin River Outfitters
653 Lowe St., Buchanan, VA 24066
540-261-7334
CanoeVirginia.net

Wilderness Canoe Company
631 James River Road
Natural Bridge Station, VA 24578
540-291-2295
WildernessCanoeCampground.com

License and Fishing Regulations

Virginia Department of Game and Inland Fisheries
P.O. Box 11104
Richmond, VA 23230
804-367-1000
DGIF.virginia.gov

Map Information

The best non-topo maps I have found are *The Upper James Atlas* and *The James River Batteau Festival Trail*. Together, they detail the entire coverage area of this book. The contents of these books helped me immeasurably in writing this book and floating the river, and I strongly recommend James enthusiasts purchasing them. The guides also include much interesting information about the region's history. **For more information:** Vacanals.org

Another useful source, especially for traveling the many back roads along the James, is the *Virginia Atlas and Gazetteer* available from:
DeLorme Mapping Company
P.O. Box 298
Freeport, Maine 04032
800-561-5105
Delorme.com

MapTech (topo maps).
I use this company's maps extensively
877-587-9004
MapTech.com

General Information

Upper James River Water Trail
UpperJamesRiverwaterTrail.com

Allegheny Highlands Blueway
AlleghanyHighlandsBlueway.com

Tourism Sources

Bedford Tourism and Welcome Center
816 Burks Hill Road
Bedford,VA 24523
540-587-5681 or 877-477-3257
VisitBedford.com

Botetourt County Office of Tourism
5 West Main Street, Suite 101
Fincastle, VA 24090
540-473-167
VisitBotetourt.com

Lexington & the Rockbridge Area Tourism
106 East Washington Street
Lexington, Virginia 24450
540.463.3777
LexingtonVirginia.com

Lynchburg Visitors Center
216 12th Street
Lynchburg, VA 24504
434-847-1811 or 800-732-5821

Nelson County Visitor Center
8519 Thomas Nelson Highway
Lovingston, VA 22949
434-263-7015 or 888-662-9400
NelsonCounty-VA.gov

Richmond Region Tourism
401 N. 3rd Street
Richmond, VA 23219
1-800-370-9004
VisitRichmondVA.com

Index

A

Allens Creek 117, 124-5
Alpine iv, 21, 47, 84-6, 89, 91-2
Alpine to Glasgow in Botetourt and
    Rockbridge counties 89
Arcadia 21, 47, 75, 80, 84-5, 87-8

B

Balcony Falls iv, 26, 93-6
Ballews Shoals 139-40
bateau 114, 122-3, 166
    era 119
    sluice 133
    times 151
bateaux (plural of bateau) 119, 165
    see also bateau
Bent Creek iv, vi, 6, 109, 125-32
Big Island iv, 97,102-3, 105-7, 156
Boatwright's Island 160-1
Bork's Shoals area 131
Boshers Dam 177
Bremo Bluff to Columbia iv, 147, 153, 158-61
Buchanan iv, v, vii, 5-6, 8, 42, 47, 63, 65, 71,
    75-6, 78-83, 85, 89, 165, 185
Buffalo Shoals area 151
Buffalo Station 132
bullhead catfish populations 5
Buzzard Islands 114

C

Cannon's Shoals 159
canoe liveries viii, 24, 27, 89, 172, 185
canoeing 26, 49, 65, 124-5, 151, 167
carp 6, 23, 55, 66
Cartersville vi, 147, 163-5, 167, 169, 171
Cashaw Dam 98
Catawba Creek 7, 65
catfish v, 1, 5-7, 20-3, 69
    anglers 52, 59, 111
    flathead 4-5, 21, 61, 69, 72, 120, 177
Chase Island Shoals 121
Chillisses' Falls 159-60
Christian Island 123
Cleveland Island 156
Cobb's Falls 162
Cobb's Island 161
Columbia iv, vi, 147, 159-60, 162-5
Columbia to Cartersville in Cumberland 163
Cowpasture River 49

Craigs Creek 57, 61, 63
Cunningham Island 133

D

Deep Creek 173
Dog Island 140-1

E

Eagle Rock iv, v, 47, 49, 57-9, 62-4, 66-7, 69
Eagle Rock to Saltpetre Cave in Botetourt
    County 63
Elk Island 166

F

floating v, 1, 24, 50, 53, 55, 68, 99, 117,
    132, 186
Freeland's Falls 129

G

Gala iv, v, 47-9, 57-9, 61
Galt's Mill and Riverville 123
Gilmore Mills 91-2
Glasgow iv, v, 26, 43, 45, 47, 89-91, 93-5, 149
Glen Wilton trip 54
Goosby Island 145
Grand Ripple Falls 139

H

Hardware River iv, 152-3
    Public Boat Landing 152
    WMA to Bremo Bluff vi, 147-9, 153-5, 157
Hatton Ferry Crossing 146
Higginbotham's Falls 117, 124
history 64, 114, 166
    nation's 49
    region's 186
Horseshoe Bend 69
Howardsville iv, vi, 109, 129, 134-5, 138-46
Howardsville to Scottsville in Albemarle 143

I

Indian Rock area 87
Iron Gate iv, v, viii, 25, 47-53, 55-6
Iron Gate to Gala in Botetourt County 49, 57

J

Jackson River 49
James River Face Wilderness Area 93
James River State Park 132

James River WMA vi, 109, 134-5, 137-9, 141
Joshua Falls iv, vi, 109-10, 114, 116-21, 124

K
Kanawha Canal 5, 43, 56, 63-4, 69, 82, 85, 87, 89, 91, 94, 119, 165
Kanawha River 56

L
ledge areas 10, 13-14
ledges 7-11, 13, 15, 18, 52, 59, 89, 91, 95, 101, 133, 143, 145, 176
Lickinghole Creek Aqueduct 173
Little Balcony Falls 95-6
Little Rock and Rock islands 145
Locher Landing 43, 89
Lynchburg vi, viii, 96, 109, 111-12, 114, 165, 186

M
Maidens' Adventure Dam 175
Maidens to Watkins Landing vi, 147, 174-5
Map Information 186
Maury River 42-3, 46, 68, 93
Micah Falls 162
muskies v, 1, 3-4, 6, 20, 23, 55, 66, 78, 92, 99, 103, 106, 111, 120

N
Narrow Passage iv, v, 47, 62-3, 69, 70-3
Narrows, The 54-5
Natural Bridge and Buchanan 89
Natural Bridge Station 185
Nine-Mile Bridge 114, 116

O
Outfitters
 Angler's Lane 111, 121, 185
 Confluence Outfitters 44, 46, 99, 103, 106, 111, 121, 185
 Dead Drift Flies 185
 Discover the James 185
 H&H Outdoors 185
 James River Reeling & Rafting 185
 James River Runners 146, 185
 Mossy Creek Fly Fishing 185
 New Angle Fishing Company 185
 New River Outdoor Company 185
 Orvis 185
 Outdoor Trails 185
 Riders Up Outfitters 185
 RockonCharters 185
 South River Fly Shop 185
 Tracy Asbury-West Virginia Outdoor Adventures 185
 Twin River Outfitters vii, 42, 44, 46, 85, 94, 185
 Wilderness Canoe Company 10, 95, 185

P
paddling 24, 36, 46, 54, 87, 96, 101, 103, 106, 122, 138, 146, 156, 166, 168, 177
Patterson's Shoals 122-3
Perkins Falls 146
Pettyjohn Island 122
Phelp's Falls. 157
photography 50, 67, 73, 115, 123, 145, 151
pictures 22, 56, 63, 73, 91-2, 95, 113, 137, 141, 146, 149, 151, 156

Q
Quarry Rapid 80-1

R
Rapids classification iv
Riverville iv, vi, 109, 117-19, 123-8
rock bass 5, 20-1, 23, 73, 85, 103-4
Rock Castle Falls 171, 173
rock islands 145
Rock Ledge Maze 141
Rockfish River 138, 141, 143
Rocky Point 85, 88

S
Salt Petre Cave 67
Scottsville iv, vi, viii, 109, 142-44, 146-50, 152, 165, 185
Scottsville to Hardware River WMA vi, 147-9, 151
Seven Islands and Big Island 156
Shallows, The 151
Six-Mile Bridge vi, 109-11, 114-15
smallmouth bass viii, 3-4, 6-7, 18, 20, 23, 49, 53, 57, 87, 94-5, 111, 120, 122, 163, 167, 177
Smith Islands 125, 127-8
Snowden iv, v, viii, 26, 42, 47, 89, 93-4, 96, 99, 103, 149
Spicer's Island 160
Springwood iv, v, 47, 70-1, 74-9
Springwood to Buchanan trip 75, 79

Squeeze, The 54
sunfish 5, 18, 20-1, 23, 85, 103-4, 159, 163, 166-7, 169, 173
Swift Island 137
Sycamore Island 139

T
Tobacco Hills Falls 96
Tod's Shoals 131
Tomlin's Shoals 146
Tourism Sources 186
Tye River 132
Tye River Dam 133

U
Upper James River v, vii, 1, 3, 42
Upper James River Water Trail vii-viii, 184, 186

V
Velvet Rock Falls 96
Virginia Canals & Navigations Society 46
Virginia's River 27

W
wade fishermen 64, 83, 135
Warren 145
water willow 49, 50, 53-5, 89, 141, 150, 171, 177
beds 23, 44-5, 55-7, 61, 65, 69, 72-3, 75, 78, 91, 99, 112-13, 115, 120, 139, 160, 182
islets 104, 135, 171, 176
Welch Rock Shoals area 132
West View 164, 171
West View to Maidens vi, 147, 170-3
Wingina vi, 6, 109, 129, 133-5, 137
Woods Island 55
Wreck Island 123-4
Wreck Island Falls 124

Y
Yogaville 138

Other books by Bruce Ingram

Fly and Spin Fishing for River Smallmouths (First E-Book Edition)

Fly and Spin Fishing for River Smallmouths is a motivating, informative guide for nature lovers of all kinds. The book delves into river bass fishing with easy-to-use tips on everything smallmouth, from lures and flies, types of cover to target, to strategies for cold and warm seasons, and much more. The book suggests enjoyable family-friendly river hobbies like canoeing, bird watching, river camping, and introducing children to the outdoors. This book also leads landowners, farmers, and adventurers in their efforts to protect our nation's waterways. From conservation easements to blueways, the author describes profitable and environmentally-enlightened government conservation programs.

Other books by Bruce Ingram

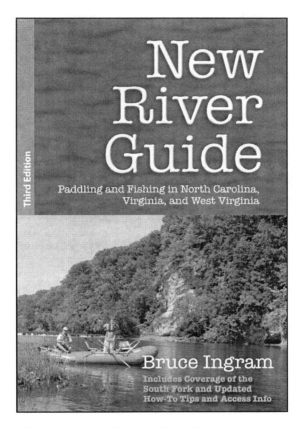

The New River Guide
(Third Edition with Updated
and Expanded Coverage)

The New River is one of the most changeable and fickle
rivers in the East—and also one of the most beautiful and
rewarding. It attracts anglers, canoeists, kayakers, rafters,
bird watchers, rock climbers and those who simply enjoy
the great outdoors. The *New River Guide* provides an
indispensable overview of this untamed and scenic
waterway as it winds through three states, including the
bucolic South Fork in North Carolina, the ridges of Virginia
and the gorges of West Virginia. This new edition for
2015 includes updated and expanded information on
favorite float trips, fishing spots, access points, bass lines
and lures, and river guides and other resources.

About Secant Publishing

Featuring classics old and new, from an independent publisher based in the heart of Maryland's historic Eastern Shore. Our vision is to connect books of enduring interest with readers of discernment. See **SecantPublishing.com** for our growing list of titles.

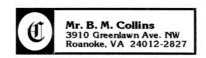

CPSIA information can be obtained
at www.ICGtesting.com
Printed in the USA
FFOW01n0131180717
37727FF

9 780990 460855